A Garden for Art

This publication has been made possible by a generous gift from
ROBERT LEHRMAN
and supported by a grant from the
SMITHSONIAN WOMEN'S COMMITTEE

A Garden for Art
Outdoor Sculpture at the Hirshhorn Museum

Valerie J. Fletcher

Hirshhorn Museum and Sculpture Garden, Smithsonian Institution, Washington, D.C.
in association with Thames and Hudson

Cover: Autumn in the Hirshhorn Museum's Sculpture Garden, with *Nymph (Central Figure for "The Three Graces")* by Aristide Maillol (no. 8).

Frontispiece: Central area of the Sculpture Garden, with works by David Smith, Alexander Calder, Henry Moore, and Gaston Lachaise (nos. 51, 49, 40, and 9).

Photographic Credits
The author wishes to thank the photographers, museums, archives, and other sources that supplied photographs of works of art in their possession and/or granted permission for works in their collections to be reproduced as illustrations. Every effort has been made to seek permission for comparative illustrations.

The following photographs were provided by Hirshhorn Museum and Sculpture Garden photographers, past and present: LEE STALSWORTH: figs. 2, 3, 23–25, 27, 32–34, 37, 41–43, and nos. 1, 2 (full view, p. 39), 3 (detail), 4, 5, 7, 9, 10, 13,17, 18, 20, 23, 27, 32, 33 (left), 38, 39, 42, 47, 49, 50, 52, 53, 54 (full view), 55, 57 (bottom), 58, 63; RICARDO BLANC: cover, frontispiece, figs. 29–31, 35, 36, 39, 40, and nos. 2 (detail, p. 38), 3 (full view), 6 (full view, detail), 8, 11, 12, 14, 19, 21, 22, 24–26, 28, 29, 30 (full view), 31, 33 (right), 34, 36, 37, 40, 41, 43–46, 48, 51, 54 (detail), 56, 57 (top), 59–62; JOHN TENNANT: figs. 19–22 and nos. 16, 35; WENDY VAIL: pp. 6–7, figs. 28, 38; and Smithsonian photographer JEFF TINSLEY, fig. 4.

Other sources of photographs are: Kröller-Müller Museum, Otterlo, The Netherlands, fig. 10; © by Philippe Halsman, New York, fig. 1; Robert E. Mates, New York, no. 15; Michio, no. 30 (detail); Ugo Mulas, Milan, Italy, fig. 5; Hugh Palmer, Banbury, England, fig. 7; photo by Ezra Stoller, © Esto, all rights reserved, fig. 26; West Stock, Seattle, fig. 8; reproduced from Charles Emile Yriarte, *Florence: Its History* (New York: Scribner and Welford, 1882), fig. 9; and Hirshhorn Museum and Smithsonian Institution archives (photographers unknown), figs. 6, 11–14, 15–18, 20–22.

Published in 1998 by the Hirshhorn Museum and Sculpture Garden, Smithsonian Institution, Washington, D.C., in association with Thames and Hudson, 500 Fifth Avenue, New York, New York 10110. No part of this book may be reproduced or transmitted in any form or by any means, electronic or mechanical, including photocopying, recording, or any information storage and retrieval system, without the permission of the publishers.

ISBN 0-500-28047-9
Library of Congress Catalog Card Number 97-61991

Edited by Jane McAllister
Designed by Thames and Hudson Ltd., London
Printed and bound in Italy by Giunti Industrie Grafiche

Contents

Acknowledgments

Many people have contributed to the creation and refinement of the Hirshhorn Museum's Sculpture Garden over the past three decades. While there are too many to acknowledge individually, I can at least thank those who have helped make this book a reality over the past several years. First and foremost must be the Hirshhorn Museum's photographers. Chief photographer Lee Stalsworth, his colleague Ricardo Blanc, and their predecessors John Tennant, Wendy Vail, and Marianne Gurley spent countless hours outdoors capturing on film myriad views of the sculptures—many more than appear in this book. My appreciation goes also to James Demetrion and Neal Benezra, director and assistant director of the museum, for their ongoing support and thoughtful reading of the manuscript. The museum's publications manager, Jane McAllister, and her predecessor, Barbara Bradley, nurtured this project through repeated challenges. A word of appreciation should also go to the Hirshhorn docents who present tours of the garden to so many visitors. Finally, we are grateful to the Smithsonian Women's Committee, which provided the start-up funds for publication, and to Robert Lehrman, the chairman of the museum's Board of Trustees, whose generosity has brought the publication to fruition. Their altrusim has created an opportunity for many people to become acquainted, through this publication, with one of the world's great sculpture collections. ■

V.J.F.

Winter in the Sculpture Garden, with Gaston Lachaise's *Standing Woman* (no. 9).

"... and Sculpture Garden"

Twenty-two verdant acres of prime Connecticut real estate provided the tranquil setting for Joseph H. Hirshhorn's splendid array of outdoor sculptures that, together with thousands of other works of art, he had amassed through four decades of enthusiastic collecting. A visitor in the early 1970s counted 144 sculptures lining the driveway and nestled among the trees and gardens of Round Hill, Mr. Hirshhorn's sumptuous Tudor-style home (fig. 1). That visitor was but one of approximately 175,000 individuals who, over the course of a decade, had made the pilgrimage to Greenwich seeking an aesthetic experience of a type that was virtually without parallel elsewhere in the country. Modern sculptors of international renown—among them Auguste Rodin, Henri Matisse, Alexander Calder, David Smith, and Henry Moore—were represented in depth and by key works.

Those masterpieces were not confined by the white walls and scientifically determined lighting of a gallery, nor by the more intimate environment of the rooms of a home. Instead, the chosen 144—surrogates for men and women and their dreams and aspirations—changed appearance from minute to minute as the sun dissolved into dusk and as darkness was brightened by the moon. The glistening surfaces caused by rain, the unpredictable and often humorous effects of snow on metal heads and shoulders, and the sudden gloom resulting from a passing cloud are experiences that the static environs of an indoor installation cannot provide. (In all fairness, however, one must note that the impact of weather is not always benign, with some of the sculptures suffering discoloration of their delicate patinas.) The green foliage of spring and summer moving restlessly in the wind formed astonishing backdrops for the sculptures in Mr. Hirshhorn's yard. The yellows, reds, and oranges of a New England autumn and the stark bare branches of winter made no less of an impression.

It should come as no surprise, therefore, that Joseph

Fig. 1   Joseph Hirshhorn's Round Hill estate in Greenwich, Connecticut, early 1970s, showing at rear left Auguste Rodin's *Burghers of Calais* (no. 2) and in foreground Antoine-Louis Barye's *Theseus Slaying the Centaur Bienor*, 1850, now housed indoors at the Hirshhorn Museum.

Hirshhorn ardently wished to transport as much as possible the feeling generated by the spacious surroundings of his home in Greenwich to the National Mall in Washington, nor is it surprising that he insisted that the words "Sculpture Garden" be coequal with "Hirshhorn Museum" as the name of the institution he founded.

In her introduction to this publication, Dr. Valerie Fletcher, Curator of Sculpture, records the various transformations that have taken place in the museum's outdoor areas over the years. Suffice it to say that the present garden and plaza are just one-fifth the acreage at Round Hill; had the same ratio of sculptures-to-space been maintained in Washington, fewer than thirty works would be on view today. Obviously, a museum committed to the enjoyment of art and to what James Smithson, founder of the Smithsonian Institution, referred to as the "diffusion of knowledge" has deemed it important to keep a relatively large number of works (about sixty-five) on view for the public's enjoyment and edification. That public, it should be noted, has swelled from the average of 17,500 persons per year at Round Hill to many times that number, making the museum and its garden one of the most heavily attended art venues in the nation.

Although many who had the pleasure of seeing the works in Connecticut miss the openness and spaciousness of that installation, others delight in the silent dialogue created by the parallels and contrasts of forms now in close proximity to one another. Nature's elements continue to take their toll, but the effects are mitigated by the specialized care provided by the museum's dedicated conservation staff. Some works have been shown in the open air for decades, with others joining them from time to time, while still others have been removed from view altogether (a few, including Alberto Giacometti's *Dog* and Henry Moore's *King and Queen*, have been installed indoors for their protection). Like the seasons, some will return; like the passing years, others will not. Ultimately, however, it was Joseph Hirshhorn's hope, as it is ours, that visitors will savor and learn from their experiences in the Sculpture Garden, just as he did. ∎

James T. Demetrion
Director

Fig. 2 Winter in the Hirshhorn Museum's Sculpture Garden, with bronzes by Auguste Rodin (nos. 2 and 3).

A Garden for Art

Welcome to the Hirshhorn Museum's Sculpture Garden, where more than sixty works of art are displayed year-round. Located on the National Mall halfway between the Washington Monument and the Capitol, the garden provides a contemplative haven in the heart of a major city (fig. 4). The sculptures installed here date from the 1880s through the 1960s, while a dozen more-recent works enhance the paved plaza around the museum building. Together these landscaped grounds form outdoor galleries enjoyed by more than 340,000 visitors each year.

The museum and garden opened in 1974, but their history began decades earlier. Although the Smithsonian Institution first wanted to establish a national museum of contemporary art in the 1930s, the Great Depression and World War II interrupted those plans. As part of a major expansion of the Smithsonian during the 1960s, the Institution's Secretary, S. Dillon Ripley, set out to acquire the world's largest and finest private collection of modern art (fig. 5), which had been amassed by multimillionaire Joseph H. Hirshhorn (1899–1981).

Fig. 3   Sculptures by Jean Ipousteguy (no. 27) and Alexander Calder (no. 49) in the Hirshhorn Museum's garden, with the Washington Monument in the background.

Fig. 4   An aerial view of the Hirshhorn Museum and Sculpture Garden, early 1980s.

Fig. 5   Round Hill estate, early 1970s, with Henry Moore's *Draped Reclining Figure* (no. 15) in foreground and Marino Marini's *Horse and Rider* (no. 16) in background.

Fig. 6   Olga and Joseph Hirshhorn flanked by Lady Bird and President Lyndon B. Johnson on May 17, 1966, the day Mr. Hirshhorn signed the agreement to donate his collection to the nation.

Wooed by many cities in the United States and abroad,[1] the Latvian-born immigrant decided in May 1966 to donate 6,600 works of art to establish a new museum for the Smithsonian in Washington, D.C. (fig. 6). Sculptures constituted nearly a fourth of Hirshhorn's gift, and from 1969 through 1981 he contributed hundreds more, for a grand total of 2,650 sculptures. A number of the large pieces had been displayed outdoors on spacious grassy terraces at his estate in Greenwich, Connecticut (see figs. 1 and 5). That spectacular array had been a major reason his collection was coveted by the Smithsonian, and both Ripley and Hirshhorn stipulated that an outdoor garden be part of the new museum.[2]

A Brief History of Sculpture Gardens

The concept of a sculpture garden as we know it today, that is, a landscaped open-air museum created specifically for the study and preservation of art, is a phenomenon that has emerged relatively recently. But it developed from distinguished predecessors in Europe, the Middle East, and Asia, dating back nearly three millennia.[3] Many cultures, from powerful empires to remote island villages, have constructed formal public spaces for ceremonial purposes and have used sculptures to illustrate or symbolize the religious, political, and

Fig. 7 Roman sculptures at the Canopus, Hadrian's Villa, Tivoli, Italy, A.D. 121–137.

artistic ideals of their societies. Most ancient sites have been destroyed or pillaged, so their sculptural character is no longer evident, but archaeologists have determined the impressive extent of some. Among the oldest were those built for Egyptian pharaohs; the Funerary Temple of Queen Hatshepsut near Thebes (c. 1480 B.C.), for example, was approached through rows of monumental stone figures. In the classical Greek civilization (650–80 B.C.), statues idealizing the gods enlivened temple complexes such as the Acropolis in Athens, while sculptures in the marketplace honored political and military leaders. The Roman empire (265 B.C.–A.D. 470) perpetuated those traditions in public places from the Forum in Rome to far-flung colonies in the Middle East. The Romans also used such sculptures to adorn private gardens, from the vast estate around Emperor Hadrian's Villa in Tivoli (fig. 7) to the small courtyards of middle-class homes in Pompeii.

After the Roman empire collapsed, however, those practices virtually ceased in Europe. For the next thousand years, the most sophisticated and extensive use of outdoor sculptures occurred elsewhere in the world. The Mayans carved narrative and symbolic reliefs and monumental images for their temples in Central America, notably at Uxmal, Yaxchilán, and Copán (A.D. 250–900) in Mexico. Throughout eastern Asia, Hindu and Buddhist

Fig. 8   Zen Buddhist rock garden in Ryōan-ji temple, Kyoto, Japan, 16th century.

cultures created countless statues and reliefs for their temple complexes, among them Borobudur (A.D. 800–900) in Java, Angkor Wat (A.D. 1100–1220) in Cambodia, and Bhuvaneshwar, Khajuraho, Kanchipuram, and Madurai (A.D. 800–1700) in India. In China powerful rulers used sculpture to enhance their status, as did the Ming emperors for their tombs near Beijing. Buddhist monks and scholars created private gardens, using rocks as nature's sculptures symbolizing philosophical and literary ideals (fig. 8).

The origins of modern sculpture gardens can be traced specifically to the Renaissance, Baroque, and Neoclassical periods from the fifteenth through the eighteenth centuries in Europe. Eager to surpass the ancient Roman prototypes, Italian connoisseurs started to build palaces with prominent spaces for statues and to incorporate sculptures in public plazas (fig. 9). The Vatican created the first outdoor sculpture museum with its landscaped Belvedere Courtyard in 1500, and collectors quickly expanded the concept. Within fifty years the Villa d'Este in Tivoli had spacious gardens with elaborate statuary and fountains. Aristocrats throughout Europe soon began to install lavish gardens where sculpture vied with horticulture for prominence. The British developed this trend into a national passion beginning in the 1560s, but French royalty set new standards with the opulent gardens at Versailles (1660–1720). Thereafter, nobility competed to have the most spectacular gardens, from Nymphenburg and Veitshöchheim in Germany to Caserta in Naples and Peterhof near Saint Petersburg. The demand for outdoor sculptures had increased so dramatically by the 1720s that a new industry emerged: minor artists carved countless prosaic imitations of classical images for use as garden decorations.

As democracy supplanted rule by the aristocracy in Europe and the Americas, many royal gardens were opened to the public during the nineteenth century. Simultaneously, as industrialization displaced agricultural economies, many towns grew into cities with public parks and plazas. Looking to precedents in Renaissance cities, Europeans and Americans commissioned bronze and stone monuments to adorn urban spaces. From the 1850s through the 1920s, people became increasingly accustomed to seeing outdoor sculptures. At first, most were classical figures symbolizing lofty ideals (such as freedom, wisdom, or courage). A second tradition gradually emerged in the form of realistic portrait statues, which became popular for commemorating political and cultural heroes (from Joan of Arc to George Washington and Simon Bolívar). In Washington, D.C., for example, where Pierre L'Enfant's city plan of 1791 created many parks, at least two dozen equestrian statues of triumphant generals remind passersby of victories in past wars. Realistic and symbolic monuments continue to be made, but a new phenomenon has caused widespread changes since the 1960s. As local and federal governments have required developers to devote a percentage of their budgets to art, hundreds of sculptures have been created for outdoor public places. Contrary to the older figurative traditions, these works have tended to be abstract in form, vivid in color, and made of modern materials, as sculptors have sought to beautify the urban setting rather than commemorate a person or event.

In a parallel development, which first materialized in the 1930s, gardens were created as outdoor museums primarily for the study of art. Some, such as the Millesgården in Stockholm and Brookgreen Gardens in South Carolina, were founded by artists and collectors. The Museum of Modern Art in New York was the most prominent institution to endorse the idea by creating a small urban courtyard. After World War II, European cities set new standards with spacious, landscaped areas for modern art, starting auspiciously in Belgium with fifteen acres for the Middelheim Open-Air Museum in Antwerp in 1950. During the 1960s an international vogue for sculpture gardens emerged; the Kröller-Müller

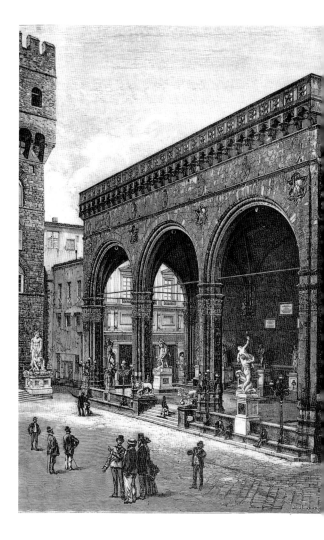

Fig. 9 Jean-François Cabarteux (late 19th century), engraving of marble sculptures in the Loggia dei Lanzi, Piazza della Signoria, Florence, Italy, 15th–16th century.

Fig. 10 Kröller-Müller Museum garden, Otterlo, The Netherlands, late 1960s, with sculpture by Marta Pan.

Museum near Otterlo in the Netherlands led the way with twenty-six acres in 1961 (fig. 10). From 1965 to 1969, sculpture gardens opened at the Maeght Foundation near Nice, the Israel Museum in Jerusalem, the Moderna Museet in Stockholm, the Louisiana Museum at Humlebaek in Denmark, and the Hakone Open-Air Museum in Japan. In the United States two gardens defined the extremes of style and size: at Storm King Art Center in suburban New York the visitor treks across rolling fields to see sculptures scattered across five hundred acres, while at the University of California at Los Angeles a small, enclosed space serves primarily as an outdoor library for academic study. Conceived in 1966–67, the Hirshhorn Museum's sculpture garden was part of this international trend.

Evolution of the Hirshhorn Museum's Garden

Although now a peaceful refuge popular with visitors, the Hirshhorn Museum's sculpture garden had a surprisingly tumultuous birth, requiring eight years from conception to completion. Secretary Ripley had initially envisioned a five-acre expanse flanked by discrete pavilions to hold smaller and fragile works.[4] From the outset, however, ideas for the new museum and garden were formulated in tandem with a much larger project championed by Lady Bird Johnson: a master plan for redeveloping twelve hundred acres of downtown Washington near the National Mall. Nathaniel Owings (of the architectural firm Skidmore, Owings & Merrill) unveiled his plan in July 1966 and was consulted regarding the Hirshhorn design. Mrs. Johnson favored Owings's idea for a rectangular sunken garden extending on a north-south axis across the three-block width of the Mall.[5]

In November 1966, Congress authorized $15 million to finance the construction of the Hirshhorn Museum and Sculpture Garden, and Gordon

Bunshaft of Skidmore, Owings & Merrill was selected as architect three months later. Although he had never designed a museum, Bunshaft was a noted collector of modern art and had recently completed the Beinecke Library building at Yale University. Consulting with the Hirshhorn Museum's first director, Abram Lerner, the architect prepared drawings and a model (figs. 11 and 12). The project, consisting of the museum building and a separate garden, would cover four-and-a-half acres. Occupying a complete city block between Independence Avenue and Jefferson Drive at the corner of Seventh Street, the museum would consist of a cylindrical building (231 feet in diameter) on a nearly square plaza (360 x 302 feet). This severely geometric design deliberately mirrored the layout, on the opposite side of the Mall, of the National Gallery of Art's proposed sculpture garden, which centered on a round pond with concentric rows of trees set in a square block between Constitution Avenue and Madison Drive (visible in fig. 12). Connecting these two symmetrical plots would be the Hirshhorn's sculpture garden, a two-acre rectangular space (586 x 142 feet) extending across the Mall. To diminish its impact on the main east-west axis of the Mall, planners decided that the garden would be seven feet below ground level and surrounded by walls three-feet high, thereby creating an enclave ten-feet deep. Bunshaft envisioned an extremely simple design: more

Fig. 11   Perspectival drawing of Gordon Bunshaft's original garden design with a large reflecting pool, 1967–69.

Fig. 12   Model of the Hirshhorn Museum showing the original garden design by Bunshaft, 1967–69.

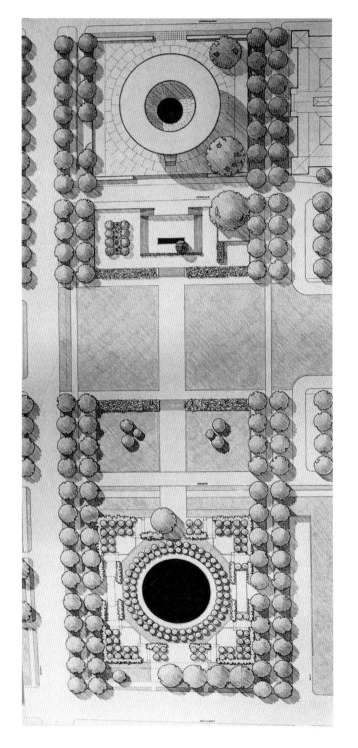

than a third of the space would consist of a long rectangular reflecting pool (506 x 60 feet), leaving a perimeter forty-feet wide for displaying the sculptures.[6] Covered in pebbles, this wide walkway would be unrelieved by any trees, bushes, or flowers. Such an austere design was consistent with Bunshaft's style for the museum building and corresponded to the Minimalist mode then fashionable among many architects and artists.

The entire plan was approved by city and federal authorities in July 1967; architectural drawings were accepted in December. After Congress provided funding in the autumn of 1968, the groundbreaking took place in January 1969. But as subsequent excavation proceeded, it prompted a public reaction. Some critics objected to the idea of having modern art occupy such a large and prominent position on the Mall, while more hostile opponents attacked Mr. Hirshhorn's character. The antagonism ranged from philistinism to politics (the Nixon administration was less enthusiastic about the museum project than its predecessor had been). A significant number of critics were quite rightly concerned that the symbolic unity and open expanse of the Mall be preserved uninterrupted from the Capitol to the Lincoln Memorial.

The controversy raged for months until, in January 1971, Congress halted work on the garden. In an insightful article published in the *Washington Star* on February 24, art critic Benjamin Forgey chastised the garden plan as too big and barren. He proposed that the garden's axis be shifted ninety degrees to run parallel to, rather than bisect, the Mall; that the garden be situated in the immediate vicinity of the museum building; that the reflecting pool be made less prominent; that the garden have terraces at several levels; and that some plantings be added to soften the setting.

In March the Smithsonian agreed to adopt most of Forgey's ideas. Bunshaft quickly completed new drawings, and the resulting compromise (fig. 13) pleased most critics. The new scheme reduced the garden's size to one-and-a-half acres (389 x 156 feet), but because the size of the reflecting pool was greatly diminished, the redesign provided only slightly less space for sculptures than did the original proposal. (The number of works, however, would still be significantly fewer than the twelve dozen sculptures displayed at Mr. Hirshhorn's estate in Greenwich.) The new plan divided the garden into terraces at several levels (see figs. 20–22). The central court with the reflecting pool was now fourteen feet below the level of the Mall, while wide flights of steps led up to two flanking terraces that joined together along the north side. The west side

Fig. 13 Schematic drawings of the original (left) and revised (right) designs for the Sculpture Garden, showing the drastic reduction in acreage.

was further divided into two smaller spaces: an enclosed square with high walls, and an open square with low walls. At street level the garden was edged on the east and west by narrow areas with stately shade trees.[7]

Although the size and arrangement had changed, Bunshaft retained the austere style of the original concept. Only a few plants were included: a group of small trees on the east terrace, a lone willow by the pool, and a shade tree in one corner. The garden floor was covered in pebbles, in the same beige tone as the concrete-aggregate walls. The overall effect emulated the purist aesthetics of Japanese Zen gardens, which had become better known in the West during the 1960s. Such gardens had been created by Buddhist monks as aids to contemplation, serenity, and insight (see fig. 8). Bunshaft thus intended the Hirshhorn's garden to serve as a tranquil and neutral setting in which the sculptures themselves would command attention, as indeed they eventually did.

On July 1, 1971, the authorities approved the new plans, and construction began soon thereafter. From late 1972 through the spring of 1974, Lerner and guest curator Douglas MacAgy worked with tiny scale-models of the sculptures, rearranging them in endless variations until they had chosen around one hundred (fig. 14).[8] In addition to featuring the most famous works, they also intended to enliven the severe architectural setting with sculptures of various colors and textures (golden brown and greenish black bronzes, silvery aluminum, and painted steel in red, black, and blue hues—all visible in the minuscule models). The central courtyard would feature Auguste Rodin's *Burghers of Calais* (the museum's most famous sculpture) and several bronzes by Henry Moore (at the time, the museum had the world's best public collection of his works). Other areas would contain geometric abstractions by David Smith and expressionist figures by European and American sculptors. Around the museum building the paved plaza would feature monumental abstract works by Alexander Calder, Tony Smith, Kenneth Snelson, and others.

Fig. 14   Guest curator Douglas MacAgy planning the placement of sculptures with tiny scale-models and photographs, November 1972.

The museum's installation staff then grappled with the practical problems of placing large sculptures in the actual garden, which began to take shape in early 1974. Designer Charles Froom and his colleagues carved life-size Styrofoam models of the sculptures (fig. 15), which were easily moved around to determine the best positions before the works of art arrived. This exercise demonstrated that the garden could not gracefully accommodate as many works as Lerner desired, and the total number was reduced, reluctantly, to seventy-five (about half the number installed on the lawns at Greenwich). In August 1974 an army of art handlers invaded Mr. Hirshhorn's estate to collect the works of art. Cranes, gantries, and even helicopters were needed to lift the largest and heaviest sculptures onto flatbed trucks for transport. Such a massive project required ingenuity by the riggers and movers, especially during certain maneuvers, such as when a large bronze hanging from a helicopter began to gyrate wildly in the breeze (fig. 16). The pilot improvised by flying over the nearby trees and lowering the piece into a sheltered clearing so that the spinning sculpture could gradually slow down enough for two men to grab it. While moving another sculpture, the handlers underestimated its stability; it fell directly onto the museum's assistant registrar, but fortunately no harm was done to the person or the sculpture. When driving their precious cargo through

Fig. 15 Full-size Styrofoam models of sculptures in the Sculpture Garden during construction, July 1974.

Fig. 16   A bronze sculpture swings in the breeze during transport by helicopter, August 1974. ▲

Figs. 17 and 18   Auguste Rodin's *Burghers of Calais* (no. 2) is installed in the Sculpture Garden, September 1974.

five states, several truckers had to take circuitous routes to avoid tunnels and underpasses too small for some sculptures.

In Washington the museum staff experienced a few dramatic moments during installation, particularly when *The Burghers of Calais* was lowered by crane (figs. 17 and 18). When the sculpture was first hoisted up from the truck and suspended over the wall to the sunken garden, the entire crane began to tip forward, threatening to topple over. Four workers immediately leapt onto the back of the crane to stabilize it until the sculpture could be returned to the truck; a larger crane was requisitioned to handle the sculpture safely. To reassemble Calder's monumental *Two Discs*, installers had to match hundreds of different-sized bolts to their proper holes (fig. 19). Despite the complexities of the entire project, not one sculpture was damaged during the removal, transit, or installation stages.[9] Today the Hirshhorn Museum is renowned for its staff's expertise in handling large, heavy, and fragile works.

Fig. 19 Alexander Calder's *Two Discs* (no. 53) is reassembled for installation on the plaza, September 1974.

The Garden's Inauguration and Redesign

The Hirshhorn Museum and Sculpture Garden opened with gala celebrations in October 1974 (figs. 20–22). The controversy surrounding the museum project slowly faded, and public response was enthusiastic. The collection of modern sculpture was said to be "without parallel in the world."[10] One critic soon noted that "many visitors to the Hirshhorn Museum (especially proud hometown Washingtonians) love it, and can't figure out why snobs and critics made such a fuss."[11] Since then the garden has attracted millions of visitors.

But the garden's shortcomings also gradually became evident: walking on the pebbled surfaces was difficult, shade was sorely missed during Washington's extremely hot summers, and access for baby strollers and wheelchairs was

Figs. 20–22 The Sculpture Garden soon after completion, early 1975, as designed by Gordon Bunshaft. The open spaces, simple walls, and use of pebbles (rather than grass) were intended to create a dramatic yet contemplative effect, like that of a Zen Buddhist "dry" garden (see fig. 8).

lacking. With no grass and few plants, the overall setting was stark, even somewhat bleak. Consequently, in 1977 landscape architect Lester Collins of the Innisfree Foundation was brought in to redesign the garden in consultation with Lerner and other Smithsonian staff.[12] Collins's plans were approved in the spring of 1978, and construction began the following year. The goals were twofold: to provide easier access by building symmetrical ramps from the Mall and to add extensive landscaping. All the sculptures had to be removed from the garden, and the space reexcavated to improve the supply of water and electricity. For its reopening in the autumn of 1981, the garden's appearance was completely revitalized (figs. 23–25). Today, sculptures rest on verdant lawns,

Figs. 23–25 The Sculpture Garden, 1981, as redesigned by Lester Collins. The large open areas have been divided into more intimate spaces, and the pebbles replaced with verdant lawns, trees, and bushes.

Fig. 26 The museum's plaza, autumn 1974, as originally designed by Gordon Bunshaft, with many sculptures but few plantings.

Fig. 27 The museum's plaza, 1993, as redesigned by James Urban, with landscaping and selected large sculptures (nos. 57 and 58).

evergreen and deciduous trees (including pines and flowering cherries) provide shade, and clematis and ivy vines cover the walls. The renovated garden proved to be more hospitable to visitors and sculptures alike.

The success of the garden's renovation prompted the museum's new director, James Demetrion, to reevaluate the plaza in the late 1980s. Since the museum's inauguration, the 2.7 acres around and under the raised building had served as a display area for dozens of large, mostly abstract, sculptures (fig. 26). Bunshaft's original plan had stipulated that the plaza be paved with gray granite and that the building be sheathed in off-white travertine marble. But budget shortfalls had forced the Smithsonian to use less-expensive concrete-aggregate for both surfaces, with the result that the plaza eventually crumbled.

In 1991 landscape architect James Urban was asked to devise a plan for the plaza. Because the plaza also serves as the roof for the museum's lower-level galleries, auditorium, and storage facilities, the site could not be excavated. With the options for planting therefore limited, Urban's design added slightly raised areas of grass and small trees on the east and west sides, following the curve of the building. The redesign also called for repaving the plaza with granite in two tones of gray, arranged in a circular pattern centered on the bronze fountain. Although the new landscaping accommodates fewer sculptures, the works benefit from the more attractive surroundings (fig. 27).

After the turbulence of its early history, the Hirshhorn Museum's garden has now become a peaceful haven. But it is not static or frozen in time; in the coming years it will continue to evolve as sculptures are added and replaced. Under careful guardianship, the works of art will continue to intrigue, challenge, and delight future generations. ■

Fig. 29 A summer's day in the garden, with Marino Marini's *Horse and Rider* (no. 16) and a group of biomorphic bronzes. ▶

Fig. 28 A winter scene, with Auguste Rodin's *Crouching Woman* (no. 1).

Notes

1 Among the suitors were the Tate Gallery in London (which offered to build a museum and twelve-acre garden in Regent's Park), the Baltimore Museum of Art (which offered to build a new wing), the cities of Zurich and Florence, and the government of Israel. See *Time*, May 20, 1966, and Barry Hyams, *Hirshhorn: Medici of Brooklyn* (New York: E. P. Dutton, 1979).

2 When Ripley proposed the acquisition of Hirshhorn's collection to the Smithsonian Regents (May 19, 1965; Smithsonian Institution Archives), he noted that "the most significant part of the collection is sculpture, which would be housed out-of-doors in a sculpture garden."

3 For further reading, see Geoffrey and Susan Jellicoe et al., *The Oxford Companion to Gardens* (Oxford and New York: Oxford University Press, 1986); Sidney Lawrence and George Foy, *Music in Stone: Great Sculpture Gardens of the World* (New York: Scala Books, 1984); Dušan Ogrin, *The World Heritage of Gardens* (London and New York: Thames and Hudson, 1993); and George Plumptre, *The Water Garden* (London and New York: Thames and Hudson, 1993).

4 In correspondence to Hirshhorn (December 18, 1964; Smithsonian Institution Archives), Ripley proposed a sculpture garden "five acres in extent, large enough to contain flanking pavilions which would protect small or fragile pieces of sculpture . . . in inclement weather."

5 Unsigned, "A Jewel for the Mall," *Time*, May 20, 1966: 88.

6 Information on the original and revised garden designs is preserved in the Smithsonian Institution Archives scattered among the papers of Secretary S. Dillon Ripley, Assistant Secretary James Bradley, and Hirshhorn Museum Director Abram Lerner, and in "The Hirshhorn Museum and Sculpture Garden Fact Sheet" (June 10, 1974; February 24, 1975; and later revised versions). Published sources include many articles in the *Washington Post*, *Washington Star*, and *New York Times*, among other newspapers, from May 1966 through November 1974. Another source is the documentary film *A Life of Its Own* made in 1974–75 (Hirshhorn Museum library).

7 The end areas along Seventh Street and the now-defunct Eighth Street, each with a row of tall elm trees, helped screen the garden from traffic and provided some shade. Because the Park Service initially retained ownership of these areas, no sculptures were installed there until the Park Service ceded them to the museum in 1993.

8 For more details, see Joanna Eagle, "A Museum Takes Shape," *ARTgallery Magazine* 16, no. 4 (January 1973): 78–80, and "An Exhibition Takes Shape," ibid., no. 5 (February 1973): 13–14, 88.

9 *New York Times*, August 13, 1974, p. 18; *Washington Post*, August 13, 1974, p. B1. My thanks go to Doug Robinson, Brian Kavanagh, Ed Schiesser, and others for recollections of those events.

10 Daniel Robbins, "The Joseph H. Hirshhorn Museum: New Seat on the Mall," *New Republic* 171, no. 22 (November 30, 1974): 25. See also Pierre Courthion, "Le plus grand musée de sculpture du monde: La collection Hirshhorn," *XXe Siècle*, n.s., 37th yr/45 (December 1975): 28–37. Vivien Raynor, "A Preview of the New Hirshhorn Museum," *New York Times*, July 14, 1974, noted that most of the masterpieces of the collection were sculptures.

11 Suzanne Stephens, "The Hirshhorn Museum and Sculpture Garden," *Artforum* 13 (February 1975): 61.

12 Collins consulted Bunshaft, who approved the renovation in a letter to Lerner (August 31, 1977; Smithsonian Institution Archives).

Outdoor Sculpture at the Hirshhorn Museum

The history of international modern sculpture from the 1880s to the present is rich and complex. Its evolution is charted by many small and midsize works displayed inside the Hirshhorn Museum, while the garden and plaza feature monumental sculptures. Their placement changes periodically; a work may be lent for exhibition elsewhere (for example, nos. 28, 43, 45, and 61 went to the White House garden for a year) or placed in storage to make space for another (like most museums, the Hirshhorn owns more objects than it is able to display at one time). In this book, the entries for individual sculptures (beginning on p. 38) are arranged in thematic groups to provide a general chronological progression of ideas and styles. The works range from traditional figures by artists such as Auguste Rodin and Aristide Maillol to abstract compositions by Alexander Calder, Kenneth Snelson, and others. An alphabetical list of the artists' names, together with their nationalities and life dates, is provided in the index (see p. 96). In the dimensions given for each work, height precedes width and depth.

The selection of sculptures for display outdoors depends in part on their materials. Only a durable medium can withstand prolonged exposure to weather and urban pollution. But even metal and stone are not as sturdy as most people imagine. Bronze sculptures are hollow, with "skins" scarcely one-quarter-inch thick. Large bronzes are assembled from several sections joined by thin welds that are invisible from the outside; the seams weaken and can break if a person, even a small child, climbs on the work of art. Fingernails, rings, buttons, and shoes cause tiny scratches that mar a sculpture's pristine surface. All sculptures also suffer from pollution, including car exhaust, acid rain, and bird droppings. Every year the surfaces of the Hirshhorn Museum's outdoor sculptures are washed (fig. 31) before being coated with an extremely thin layer of microcrystalline wax (or sometimes oil or paint for steel sculptures). Such protective coatings are quickly eroded by the natural oil in human hands; even a light touch can leave the metal exposed to the elements. Visitors are invited to look at and enjoy the sculptures, but touching them in any way is not permitted. With the public's cooperation, these works of art will be preserved for future generations.

Fig. 30 Springtime in the Sculpture Garden, with Henry Moore's *Upright Motive No. 1* (no. 35) in the foreground.

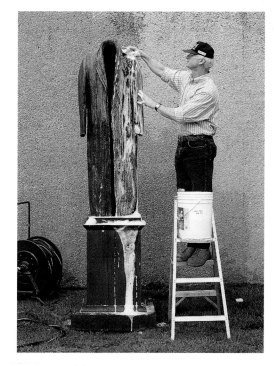

Fig. 31 Hirshhorn Museum sculpture conservator Lee Aks washes Judith Shea's *Post-Balzac* (no. 61) to remove dirt and pollutants before adding a protective wax coating.

Until recently, the most frequently used materials for outdoor sculpture have been bronze and stone. The technique of bronze casting, developed independently by various cultures around the world, has existed for more than five thousand years. For many centuries the method was usually limited to producing only one bronze from a clay, plaster, or wax original. The original was normally destroyed in the process of casting, leaving the bronze as a unique work of art. The sculptor would take great care in finishing the surface: smoothing rough areas and adding details (chasing), and using chemicals and heat to achieve a surface coloration (patina). But in the nineteenth century, especially in France, technology was developed to allow sculptors to produce multiple casts. Foundries could make precise molds that did not destroy the original; the molds could be reused or remade when another cast was desired. Sculptors could thus make several identical bronzes, with each one considered an original work of art equal in stature to the other casts. Moreover, the sculptor could leave instructions with the highly skilled foundry technicians to do the chasing and create the patina, so the artist did not need to finish each cast personally. Although the improved technology meant that more people could own sculptures, problems also arose: when too many casts were made mechanically, quality declined and some casts were created without the artist's knowledge or permission.

Fig. 32   View looking west in the Sculpture Garden, with bronzes by Francisco Zuñiga (no. 30) and Gaston Lachaise (no. 9).

Most sculptors learned to limit their editions to a dozen or fewer and to forbid posthumous casting. Some sculptors, however, chose to allow heirs to make casts long after the artist's death. Rodin, for example, bequeathed his plasters to the French government for the establishment of a museum, which he authorized to make up to twelve casts of each work. *The Burghers of Calais* can thus be seen in Calais, Copenhagen, Brussels, London, Washington, Paris, Tokyo, and elsewhere. By the 1950s most sculptors marked the number on each cast, usually near the bottom with the signature or foundry mark. Hence, "2/6" means the second from an edition of six (although some artists made an extra copy, which they numbered zero).

Some sculptures dating from the 1880s to the 1940s on view in the Hirshhorn Museum's garden were created as monuments, intended to commemorate a historic event or person or to decorate a park or other public place. Unlike paintings, which can be made privately at little expense, the creation of large sculptures often requires several assistants and expensive metalworking techniques, such as casting bronze or cutting and welding steel. Monumental works have therefore usually depended on financial subsidies in the form of commissions from governments, institutions, and wealthy patrons—a conservative clientele that has tended to favor conventional styles and subjects and to discourage change and novelty. Innovative artists usually introduced new ideas in small compositions in their studios; their concepts sometimes took years or even decades to find expression in large outdoor works intended for the public. Thus, sculptures at the Hirshhorn range from subtle variations on past traditions to those that are assertively modern in subject, style, and material. ■

Fig. 33　A spring day in the garden, with sculptures by Dimitri Hadzi (no. 36) and Henry Moore (no. 41).

The Human Figure: Traditions Transformed

From time immemorial the human figure has been the preeminent subject for art, particularly among European and European-influenced cultures. The classical Greeks defined and perfected the depiction of male and female nudes as idealized embodiments of religious, political, cultural, and aesthetic values. For more than twenty-five hundred years, artists perpetuated and refined classical symbolism, notably in the Renaissance, when criteria were established for figural forms, proportions, poses, and subjects. But by the late nineteenth century the images had become overused. The annual Paris salon exhibitions were crowded with hundreds of sculptures in an academic, classicizing style—often technically competent but repetitive and uninspiring. As that century came to its end, however, a few sculptors revitalized and redirected traditional symbolism to express ideas that were pertinent and accessible to modern audiences. Auguste Rodin, in particular, believed that the artist should infuse each subject with a personal, even passionate, interpretation. Stimulated by his example, many sculptors from the 1890s through the present day have developed expressionist styles. Such artists tend to portray the human figure as distraught, suffering, or struggling in an arduous world, and the sculptures often have rough, distorted, or scarred surfaces. Other artists such as Aristide Maillol and Henri Matisse have emphasized tranquil and reassuring subjects, with calm poses, clear contours, and smooth surfaces. In the works exhibited here, each artist hoped to convey an idea or mood, using the body as a vehicle for that expression. ∎

Fig. 35   Detail from *The Burghers of Calais*.

Fig. 34   Auguste Rodin's *Burghers of Calais* (no. 2), with Giacomo Manzù's *Self-Portrait with Model at Bergamo* (no. 14) in background.

1 AUGUSTE RODIN
Crouching Woman, 1880–82, cast 1962

Bronze [3/12], 37½ x 27⅝ x 24¼ in. (95.1 x 70.2 x 61.5 cm)
Gift of Joseph H. Hirshhorn, 1966 (66.4342)

In 1880, Rodin received his first public commission—a pair of enormous bronze doors depicting scenes from Dante's *Inferno*—intended for the Musée du Louvre in Paris. He became so obsessed with the project that he continued to work on *The Gates of Hell* until his death nearly forty years later. He also revised and enlarged certain figures as independent works, notably *The Thinker* and *Crouching Woman*. Seen alone, the figure no longer has a specific subject, but the pose expresses a forceful state of mind. In *Crouching Woman* the torsion is so physically difficult that it conveys a feeling of corporeal pain, which in turn implies a state of profound emotional or psychological suffering. The exposure of female genitals defied contemporary social standards of modesty, but Rodin did not present the figure as enticing or seductive. Rather, with her averted head and closed eyes, she appears utterly withdrawn. By pointing to her breast (a traditional gesture symbolizing maternal love), she indicates her willingness, even amidst torment, to nurture.

2 AUGUSTE RODIN
The Burghers of Calais, 1884–89, cast 1953–59

Bronze [8/12], 79⅜ x 80⅞ x 77⅛ in. (201.7 x 205.4 x 195.8 cm)
Gift of Joseph H. Hirshhorn, 1966 (66.4340). See also figs. 34 and 35.

In 1884 the French town of Calais commissioned Rodin to create a memorial honoring heroes of the Hundred Years' War. In 1347 the town had surrendered to the English king Edward III after an eleven-month siege. To preserve the town from being pillaged, six citizens (burghers) volunteered to leave Calais barefoot, tied by rope at the neck, to present Edward with the key to the city and then to serve as permanent hostages. Unlike traditional monuments, which showed heroes striding forward proudly, Rodin depicted individuals who were profoundly anguished at the thought of never seeing their homes and families again. Breaching artistic conventions, Rodin distorted the figures to express emotional trauma: the enlarged hands and feet bring attention to their melancholy gestures and faltering steps; the tautened muscles convey a sense of suppressed physical stress; and the deeply sunken eyes and furrowed brows eloquently express heart-rending torment. The novel idea that heroic deeds are performed at great sacrifice by average people infuriated the authorities in Calais, who reluctantly accepted the monument in 1895 but refused to

place it in front of the town hall until 1925. Nevertheless, Rodin's vision set a precedent for later memorials that would commemorate the efforts of ordinary soldiers, such as Felix de Weldon's *Iwo Jima Memorial* (1954) and Maya Lin's *Vietnam Veterans Memorial* (1982) in Washington, D.C.

3   AUGUSTE RODIN
Monument to Balzac, 1891–98, cast 1965–66

Bronze [6/12], 106 x 43 x 50⅜ in. (269.2 x 109.2 x 127.9 cm)
Gift of Joseph H. Hirshhorn, 1966 (66.4344). See also fig. 2.

After redefining the concept of war memorials in *The Burghers of Calais*, Rodin tried to revitalize public portraiture. In 1891 he was asked to sculpt a monument to Honoré de Balzac (1799–1850), who had developed the modern novel to new levels of subtlety and sophistication. Rejecting traditional norms that required realistic details and "Sunday best" clothes, Rodin sought an innovative image. In dozens of preliminary studies he struggled to translate Balzac's homely face and potbellied physique into an inspirational vision. Finally, he decided to use the monk's robe, which Balzac habitually wore while writing, to camouflage the body and force attention up to the head. By exaggerating the craggy facial features, deep-set eyes, and

unkempt hair, Rodin showed the arrogant, libidinous storyteller in a moment of intense concentration. Rodin was sorely disappointed when the monument was rejected and critics compared it to a penguin and a sack of coal. A bronze cast was not installed in Paris until two decades after the artist's death.

4 EMILE-ANTOINE BOURDELLE
The Great Warrior of Montauban, 1898–1900, cast 1956

Bronze [3/10], 73¼ x 62 x 24⅛ in. (186 x 157.2 x 61.3 cm)
Gift of Joseph H. Hirshhorn, 1966 (66.593)

In 1897, Bourdelle's hometown of Montauban in southwest France commissioned him to create a memorial to those who had died in the Franco-Prussian War of 1870. Following traditional norms, he sculpted a male figure in combat reaching back with one arm to protect a woman who symbolized France. Dissatisfied, Bourdelle edited the composition into this one partial figure, which gained energy from Rodin's ideas about using extra-large hands and taut musculature. The figure's physique refers to ancient Greek sculptures of warriors (such as the *Farnese Hercules* in the Vatican), while the pose alludes to the famous revolutionary scene *The Marseillaise* (1835–36), sculpted by François Rude for the Arc de Triomphe in Paris. By emphasizing the dramatic silhouette of the head, arm, and enormous splayed hand, Bourdelle powerfully evoked his country's desperate effort to hold back the tide of an invading army. That endeavor failed, but this image captures the heroic determination of defenders in wars throughout history.

5 AUGUSTE RODIN

Walking Man, 1899–1900, enlarged 1905, cast 1962

Bronze [5/12], 84¼ x 61⅝ x 28⅞ in. (214 x 155.8 x 73.1 cm)
Gift of Joseph H. Hirshhorn, 1966 (66.4343). See also fig. 25.

As Rodin achieved increasing fame in his later years, he was convinced that sculptures of partial human figures could be more expressive than the whole (like the broken sculptures of Greek and Roman antiquity so widely admired in museums). By 1900 he wanted to suggest a new kind of public sculpture that did not refer to a specific event or person. He resurrected the plaster studies for an earlier work, *Saint John the Baptist* from 1877–78, which portrayed the prophet in realistic detail. In reassembling the pieces into a new sculpture, Rodin used such force in reattaching the torso to the legs and removing the head and arms that he created harsh surface gouges. Those losses and blemishes suggest that the figure has survived physical torment, yet he still strides forward purposefully. This new and powerful symbol for humanity's determined perseverance in the face of adversity inspired sculptors such as Maillol in 1905 (see no. 6) and Giacometti in the 1940s. Many other artists developed the idea of the partial figure into a wide array of sculptures, ranging from Constantin Brancusi's highly refined heads and torsos to expressionist fragments like Saul Baizerman's *Miner* (no. 13) and Raymond Mason's *Falling Man* (no. 24).

6 ARISTIDE MAILLOL
Action in Chains: Monument to Louis-Auguste Blanqui,
1905–06, cast 1969

Bronze [6/6], 84¼ x 37¼ x 40¼ in. (213.9 x 94.3 x 102.1 cm)
Museum Purchase with Funds Provided under the Smithsonian
Institution Collections Acquisitions Program, 1979 (79.10). See also fig. 23.

This sculpture honors a now-forgotten French revolutionary and
political activist who had vehemently opposed the monarchist
government of Napoleon III. For a half-century, Louis-Auguste
Blanqui (1805–1881) campaigned for a democratic republic with
a socialist economy—a radical agenda that was to earn him
repeated imprisonment. Despite more than thirty-five years
spent in prison, he built an influential political party. Even after
his death, his courage inspired many in the Third Republic, and
in 1904 the Blanquist party commissioned a monument for his
hometown of Puget-Théniers in southwest France. Referring to
Greco-Roman traditions, Maillol used a female nude as a symbol

of victory, but he subtly adapted
some of Rodin's innovations
(notably the muscular physique
of *Crouching Woman*, no. 1, and
the pose of *Walking Man*, no. 5)
to convey Blanqui's inspirational
power. The figure's hands are
tied behind her back to
symbolize Blanqui's long
imprisonment, but the forceful
figure cannot be restrained.

7 HENRI MATISSE
The Back, I–IV, 1909–31, cast 1959–60

Bronze [0/10], each 74¾ x 47 x 8⅜ in. (189.9 x 119.3 x 21.2 cm)
Gift of Joseph H. Hirshhorn, 1966 (66.3461–3464)

In the early twentieth century many innovative artists in Europe lost interest in historic subject matter and preferred to concentrate instead on matters of style. In 1909, Matisse sculpted a large relief of a muscular female nude in a torsional pose that paid tribute to Rodin's art. In 1913, when Matisse had developed his own style, he made a revised version with simplified forms emptied of Rodin's emotional intensity. In 1916–17, Matisse transformed the image again, using severely condensed geometric forms, and he pursued that tendency further in the last version in 1930–31. Thus, by relying on progressively more massive proportions and greater abstraction of form, Matisse created a powerful expressiveness that exists without the symbolic narratives of his predecessors. This purely aesthetic expression would be pursued by many artists from the 1910s through the 1930s (see works by Lipchitz and Archipenko, nos. 31 and 45).

8   ARISTIDE MAILLOL
Nymph (Central Figure for "The Three Graces"),
1930, cast by 1953

Bronze [edition of 8], 60⅞ x 24½ x 18¾ in. (154.5 x 62.3 x 47.4 cm)
Gift of Joseph H. Hirshhorn, 1966 (66.3203). See also cover.

Maillol strove to create public sculptures featuring a modern
version of classical traditions. In Greek mythology the Graces
were attendants to Aphrodite, goddess of love; they
disseminated sweetness, joy, and fertility. In springtime they
mingled with nymphs to dance in celebration of the budding
of nature, which makes the subject particularly appropriate for
gardens. Famous sculptures of the three Graces were made by
an anonymous Greek artist (4th century B.C.) and by the Italian
Neoclassicist Antonio Canova (1815–17). Maillol's version shows
the Graces holding hands, about to start dancing. The artist
then selected the central figure as a separate *Nymph* sculpture,
seen here. In contrast to the contorted poses and emotional
angst of Rodin's figures, Maillol sought serenity in his nudes,
with clear contours, elegant poses, and smooth surfaces.

9   GASTON LACHAISE
Standing Woman, 1932, cast 1981

Bronze [3/6], 88¼ x 44¾ x 25⅜ in. (224 x 113.6 x 64.3 cm)
Museum Purchase with Funds Provided under the Smithsonian Institution
Collections Acquisitions Program, 1981 (81.2). See also pp. 6–7 and fig. 32.

Lachaise used the female nude in art to express symbolically
his concept of woman as the source of physical and emotional
strength, warmth, sensuality, and vitality in the modern era.
Partly inspired by prehistoric stone carvings of fertility
goddesses, Lachaise also paid homage to his strong-minded
and amply proportioned wife, Isabel Nagle. *Standing Woman*
emanates pride, confidence, and serenity, to such an extent that
the sculpture is often known as "Heroic Woman." Lachaise's
image contrasted markedly with a thin-bodied look in vogue
among women in the 1920s and diverged as well from the
traditional proportions of the human figure in sculpture (as
exemplified by no. 8). Lachaise also resisted the emerging trend
among artists for geometric abstraction (as seen in Lipchitz's
Figure, no. 31).

10 HENRI LAURENS

Maternity, 1932

Bronze [1/6], 21 x 55⅞ x 24 in. (53.1 x 142 x 60.9 cm)
Gift of Joseph H. Hirshhorn, 1966 (66.2909)

11 JACOB EPSTEIN

The Visitation, 1926, cast 1955

Bronze [edition of 9], 65⅛ x 20⅞ x 18⅞ in. (165.3 x 53.1 x 47.9 cm)
Gift of Joseph H. Hirshhorn, 1966 (66.1786)

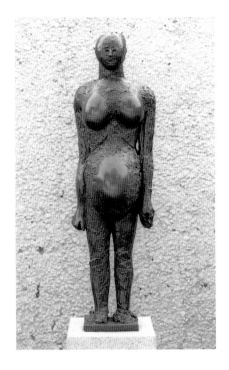

12 PABLO PICASSO

Pregnant Woman (First Version), 1950

Bronze [2/2], 41¼ x 12⅝ x 9⅝ in. (104.7 x 32.1 x 24.4 cm)
Gift of Joseph H. Hirshhorn, 1972 (72.232)

From prehistoric times through many eras, when society defined women primarily as procreators and mothers, pregnancy was an honored theme in art. In the nineteenth century, Victorian prudery banished references to bodily functions, but modern artists returned to the subject. Laurens's *Maternity*, which derived from a sculpture by Matisse, places the woman's abdomen at the center of the sculpture. Epstein sculpted the biblical subject of Mary in *The Visitation*, which shows her as humbly resigned to her fate, wringing her hands and a bit frightened by the responsibility of bearing the son of God. Picasso's *Pregnant Woman* expressed his desire to have a third child with his mistress, Françoise Gilot. He emphasized the physicality of pregnancy by making the distended breast and belly areas smoothly polished, like tautly stretched skin. Henry Moore also explored the subject (see no. 20).

13 SAUL BAIZERMAN
The Miner, 1939–45

Hammered copper with iron supports on concrete base
83⅞ x 45⅛ x 39⅛ in. (213 x 114.5 x 99.4 cm)
Gift of Joseph H. Hirshhorn, 1972 (72.18)

Inspired by Rodin's sculptures of heroic nudes (see nos. 1 and 5), Baizerman created *The Miner* in tribute to hardworking, poverty-stricken miners, who had fueled the great industrial growth of the United States for decades without sharing fully in the benefits. Intended as a public monument, *The Miner* presents the torso of an anonymous laborer toughened by years of physical effort. Empathizing with workers, Baizerman used a strenuous technique: over a six-year period he manually hammered a large flat sheet of copper until he had forced it into deep relief with a shimmering surface. He hoped that the marks generated by his method would demonstrate how the act of labor can be an essential part of art.

14 GIACOMO MANZÙ
Self-Portrait with Model at Bergamo, 1942

Bronze [1/1], 52¼ x 38⅝ x 10⅝ in. (132.7 x 98.1 x 25.7 cm)
Gift of Joseph H. Hirshhorn, 1966 (66.3293)

Through his choice of subject for this sculpture, Manzù expressed his hopes and dreams while struggling to survive in Italy during World War II. This self-portrait shows him painting (because metals were too scarce for sculpture) and wearing a coat and hat (because fuel was lacking to heat his studio). As Europe fell in ruins, Manzù yearned for a better future, and although he worked alone without a model, he portrayed a woman posing for him. The physical perfection of the nude, whose body stands out from the background, was a personal symbol representing his desire for renewal and a better life beyond the destruction and horror of 1942. As in Maillol's *Nymph* (no. 8), the idealized anatomy, solid forms, and smooth surfaces of Manzù's nude convey a serene effect.

Postwar Angst and Humanism

In the aftermath of World War II and throughout the Cold War that followed, many artists in Europe and the Americas created disturbing images that evoked the sufferings of war and expressed the pervasive anxieties of the era. After many years of interest in creating beautiful forms for their own sake, including the development of sophisticated abstract styles (see pp. 61–89), many sculptors returned to the expressive power of the human figure. Most of the new figurative works did not allude directly to specific historical events. Instead, artists sought timeless and universal messages about fear, cruelty, trauma, and devastation. Sculptors such as Alberto Giacometti, Marino Marini, Germaine Richier, and others referred back to Rodin's concepts of using dramatic poses and distorted anatomy to create their pessimistic images. These artists often roughened or gouged the surfaces of their bronze figures to suggest physical or emotional abuse.

In contrast, other postwar figurative artists wanted to reaffirm humanist values, such as the dignity, courage, and decency of individuals and the enduring qualities of society and culture. Henry Moore, for example, adapted his earlier experience with abstract style to create organic figures that convey a sense of solidity, composure, and permanence. By fusing the human body with forms from the natural world, he created symbols for the renewal and continuation of life. Other artists, such as Giacomo Manzù and Francisco Zuñiga, depicted the quiet strength of anonymous people in the world around them, from priests in Italy to poverty-stricken peasants in Mexico. ■

Fig. 37   Henry Moore's *Seated Woman* (no. 20).

Fig. 36   An array of figurative bronzes dating from the 1880s through the 1970s (left to right, nos. 46, 30, 18, 2, 29, and 14).

15 HENRY MOORE
Draped Reclining Figure, 1952–53, cast 1956

Bronze [2/4], 40⅞ x 66⅝ x 34⅛ in. (100.5 x 169 x 86.5 cm)
Gift of Joseph H. Hirshhorn, 1966 (66.3634). See also fig. 5.

During World War II, while making drawings of people in London's bomb shelters, Moore became interested in how clothing either hides or accentuates the body. When visiting Greece in 1951, he was inspired by the robed figures of classical sculptures. He subsequently made a series of small studies of a draped reclining female figure. Those works culminated in this monumental sculpture, which deliberately evokes the recumbent figures of river deities created for the pediment of the Parthenon (permanently displayed in the British Museum in London). The solid forms and squared-off pose also refer to ancient Pre-Columbian sculptures of the rain god Chac-Mool, which Moore had admired since the 1920s.

16 MARINO MARINI
Horse and Rider, 1952–53

Bronze [edition of 4], 82¼ x 47 x 77¾ in. (208.8 x 119.2 x 197.5 cm)
Gift of Joseph H. Hirshhorn, 1966 (66.3345). See also figs. 5 and 29.

In European civilization since at least the time of the Roman empire, the image of an equestrian figure had traditionally been used to portray a victorious general or king. But after World War II, Marini questioned the validity of such confidence, depicting instead a figure who is no longer in control of his horse, himself, or his fate. Here, man and beast strain their heads upward as if imploring the heavens for help or forgiveness or asking the aching question "Why?" Marini applied acids to the bronze surface, creating rough areas that suggest the horse and rider had experienced physical torment.

17 GIACOMO MANZÙ
Standing Cardinal, 1954

Bronze [1/1], 66¼ x 22⅞ x 18 in. (168.3 x 58 x 45.6 cm)
Gift of Joseph H. Hirshhorn, 1966 (66.3270)

During his childhood in Bergamo, Italy, Manzù lived in an environment permeated by Roman Catholicism (his father was a sacristan at the local church). The young Giacomo was impressed by the clergy's elaborate vestments and as a teenager was apprenticed to a craftsman who carved figures of angels for use as religious decorations. As an adult, Manzù began to sculpt a series of cardinals in 1938 and continued for more than thirty years. Each is different in size and details, but they are not portraits of specific individuals. Rather, they are generic images of a serene figure of authority, unchanged through centuries of turmoil.

18 GIACOMO MANZÙ
Young Girl on a Chair, 1955

Bronze [1/6], 45 x 23¾ x 43¼ in. (114.2 x 60.3 x 109.7 cm)
Gift of Joseph H. Hirshhorn, 1966 (66.3290). See also fig. 36.

Manzù began depicting adolescent girls in the early 1930s and continued the subject episodically. He was fascinated by young models who, despite the turbulence of the times, appeared to remain uncorrupted by adult concerns. This work portrays Francesca Blanc, daughter of a friend of the artist's, seated on a kitchen chair. The girl posed patiently for Manzù during many sessions, allowing him to capture her ingenuous youthfulness.

19 GERMAINE RICHIER
Grain, 1955

Bronze [edition of 11], 57 x 13¾ x 13½ in. (144.8 x 35 x 34.3 cm)
Gift of Joseph H. Hirshhorn, 1966 (66.4240)

After World War II, Richier's sculptural style and ideas changed dramatically. She began to merge human bodies with animal, insect, and vegetable shapes to create unnaturally mutated, hybrid creatures. Often appearing mangled or flayed, with exposed skeletons, her figures serve as haunting reminders of past destruction and harbingers of impending death. The title of this work refers to wheat, corn, or rice, but the figure's forms and pose suggest a grasshopper or locust—that is, a destroyer of crops, a plague that can bring famine.

20 HENRY MOORE
Seated Woman, 1956–57

Bronze [0/6], 62 x 56¼ x 41⅜ in. (157.5 x 142.8 x 105.1 cm)
Joseph H. Hirshhorn Bequest, 1981 (86.3277). See also fig. 37.

Throughout his career, Moore sculpted many seated female figures, sometimes mothers with children. In conjunction with a commission from UNESCO in the mid-1950s, he spent over two years creating compositions intended to honor motherhood. Some portray a woman with one or two small children, but here Moore presents an evocative image of pregnancy as a symbol of potentiality. Although Moore later said that he was partly inspired by a memory of his mother, *Seated Woman* has no identity or narrative. Her somewhat precarious pose conveys an undertone of uncertainty, but the regal posture of her upper body and head suggests an ancient goddess, strong and proud.

21 FRITZ WOTRUBA
Figure with Raised Arms, 1956, cast 1957

Bronze [1/2], 75⅛ x 20 x 15⅛ in. (190.6 x 50.8 x 38.4 cm)
Gift of Joseph H. Hirshhorn, 1966 (66.5588)

Although the Cubist movement ended in the 1920s, its
influence continued for many years. Wotruba believed in the
strength and serenity of simple geometric forms, which he used
in art to discipline the unruly human body. Commissioned for a
church in Salzburg, Austria, this figure appropriately has arms
raised up to heaven in a gesture of supplication. The original
sculpture was carved in limestone, which Wotruba then had
cast in bronze. The surface texture of the Hirshhorn's statue
thus retains the "feel" of stone.

22 ALBERTO GIACOMETTI
Monumental Head, 1960

Bronze [1/6], 37 x 11¾ x 14⅜ in. (94 x 29.7 x 36.3 cm)
Gift of Joseph H. Hirshhorn, 1966 (66.2042)

Haunted by the specter of death after World War II, Giacometti
sculpted gaunt figures with staring eyes. The rough, gouged
surfaces of his bronzes evoke the ravages of physical abuse, as
if the flesh had been burnt or flayed. The largest of many
portraits depicting Giacometti's younger brother Diego, this
head was created from memory, presenting only the most
essential features. It was partly inspired by the colossal
Byzantine stone *Head of the Emperor Constantine*, which
Giacometti had recently seen in the Capitoline Museum, Rome.

23 ELISABETH FRINK
Fallen Bird Man, 1961

Bronze [1/3], 21⅝ x 62⅞ x 34⅜ in. (54.7 x 159.5 x 87.2 cm)
Gift of Joseph H. Hirshhorn, 1966 (66.1970)

This sculpture alludes to the Greek myth of Icarus, son of Dedalus, the first man to create wings for human flight. Although the wings allowed the two men to transcend the limitations of gravity and geography, they also led to tragedy. When Icarus flew too close to the sun, the wax wings melted and he plummeted to his death. For many artists during the 1950s and 1960s, the Icarus myth seemed an appropriate metaphor for modern humanity, which had such high hopes in the early twentieth century and then fell so appallingly short of those ideals. Frink captured here that impression of falling helplessly to disaster, limbs flailing in vain for support. As in Giacometti's *Monumental Head* (no. 22), the surface of Frink's sculpture conveys a suggestion of catastrophe by appearing gouged and scorched.

24 RAYMOND MASON
Falling Man, 1962

Bronze [5/6], 48¼ x 102⅛ x 27⅝ in. (122.6 x 259.4 x 70 cm)
Gift of Joseph H. Hirshhorn, 1980 (80.35)

While visiting a quarry, Mason was inspired by the muscular backs of men working there, bent and strained by their labors. Viewed as a sequence of movement from left to right, the three torsos in this sculpture are understood as one, falling irrevocably. The allegory of collapse and perhaps defeat or death is reinforced by the exposed bones and muscles.

25 LEONARD BASKIN
Hephaestus, 1963, cast 1965

Bronze [3/4], 65⅝ x 25½ x 24⅛ in. (166.5 x 64.6 x 61.3 cm)
Gift of Joseph H. Hirshhorn, 1966 (66.394)

This sculpture refers to the god in classical mythology who brought fire to humanity. By enabling man to forge metal, Hephaestus launched the steady development of technological advances from antiquity onward. In Greek society he became the patron of all metalworkers, such as toolsmiths, armorers, and mechanics. Usually portrayed with the robust torso and arms of a smithy, Hephaestus was also lame, which led humans to mock him despite his selfless contribution to civilization. The Hirshhorn's statue has a potbellied physique, which Baskin intended as a sly reference to Rodin's *Monument to Balzac* (no. 3). That work had originally consisted of a corpulent male nude, but Rodin added the robe in 1898 in order not to offend public standards of modesty. Baskin believed the public was ready for a realistic image in 1963.

26 PAUL SUTTMAN
Resting, 1965

Bronze [1/1], 65¼ x 27⅝ x 24 in. (165.6 x 70 x 61 cm)
Gift of Joseph H. Hirshhorn, 1972 (72.284)

While many artists turned to abstract styles during the 1950s and 1960s, others insisted on the importance of the human figure as the most familiar and accessible image for conveying ideas and emotions. Suttman particularly admired Rodin's evocative sculptures and sought to impart a contemplative quality to his own works. He preferred to base his sculptures on real people; in this case, the model was probably the artist's second wife, Elisse. Here, the young woman leans against a door or wall, lost in thought. She betrays no strong emotion, but the downcast eyes and the hand absently clutching her gown suggest exhaustion or a discreet anxiety. The artist's indefinite modeling of her countenance further obscures any specific narrative and conveys instead a mood of gentle and somewhat mysterious introspection.

27 JEAN IPOUSTEGUY
Man Passing through the Door, 1966

Bronze [4/9], 77¼ x 54¼ x 46½ in. (196.3 x 137.6 x 117.9 cm)
Gift of Joseph H. Hirshhorn, 1972 (72.152). See also fig. 3 for rear view.

This sculpture presents the bizarre image of a three-armed man whose body passes through a closed door. The discrepancy between reality and illusion, between physical and metaphysical domains, surprises viewers and invites speculation about possible meanings. Another mystery is posed by the canine head emerging from one side of the door: is it a faithful pet or an ominous harbinger of death? With the figure's tense musculature and forceful posture implying a serious purpose, the sculpture offers a metaphor for humanity's pressing forward into new realms of endeavor and awareness despite obstacles.

28 WILLEM DE KOONING

Seated Woman on a Bench, 1972, cast 1976

Bronze [edition of 10], 37¾ x 36 x 34⅜ in. (95.9 x 91.9 x 87.4 cm)
Joseph H. Hirshhorn Bequest, 1981 (86.1364)
Photographed in The White House garden

29 WILLEM DE KOONING

Clamdigger, 1972, cast 1976

Bronze [4/10], 59½ x 29⅝ x 23¾ in. (151.1 x 75.2 x 60.3 cm)
Joseph H. Hirshhorn Bequest, 1981 (86.1363). See also fig. 36.

Known primarily as an Abstract Expressionist painter, de Kooning started sculpting during a visit to Italy in 1969. His art never emphasized a figure's sensuality; rather, he extended the expressionist mode introduced by Rodin into an art of unglamorous distortion. De Kooning used his own physical movement to generate style: wearing heavy gloves, he vigorously twisted and kneaded the clay into energetic surfaces. The lively effect of *Seated Woman on a Bench* contrasts with the serenity of Moore's *Seated Woman* (no. 20).

30 FRANCISCO ZUÑIGA
Seated Yucatán Woman, 1973

Bronze [3/4], 41½ x 35⅜ x 44⅞ in. (102.9 x 89.7 x 112.7 cm)
Gift of Joseph H. Hirshhorn, 1976 (76.93)

Like several earlier artists (see Lachaise's *Standing Woman*, no. 9), Zuñiga created images of women who embody strength, love, and fecundity. Living in Mexico, he particularly admired the peasant women of Central America, whom he perceived as noble descendants of the great Pre-Columbian cultures. Zuñiga's sculptures honor these women, who manage to survive the hardships of poverty. An emblem of human stoicism, *Seated Yucatán Woman* portrays a Mayan whose body has become heavy and exhausted from years of childbearing and hard work. Resting a moment from her labors, she has fallen asleep; the gesture of one arm fallen to the ground poignantly expresses

her lassitude. Despite the hardships of her daily life, her face in repose has a serene dignity and grace. Her image symbolizes the millions of anonymous women whose appearance and lifestyle contrast starkly with the artificial icons that dominate modern mass media.

Abstraction: A New Language for a New Era

In the early years of the twentieth century, people recognized that the modern era would be dramatically different from the past. Life was changing with astounding speed as democracy and middle-class values superseded aristocracies, mass-production displaced handicraft, and technological inventions promised an era of ease and affluence. Progressive artists believed that art needed to change radically to keep pace with, or even accelerate, such sweeping redefinitions of life and society. Rejecting traditional subjects and styles as belonging to a defunct past, many painters and sculptors began to concentrate on creating forms for their own sake rather than portraying recognizable subjects, which became increasingly the domain of photography. Innovative artists reduced or eliminated representation and drastically revised the definitions of art and beauty to suit the tumult and complexity of the contemporary world. In the 1910s and 1920s the avant-garde in Europe developed new styles of abstraction, believing that nonrepresentational forms offered a visual language that could transcend national, ethnic, and cultural borders. By the 1930s those styles had spread to the Americas and beyond, and by the 1950s they had become internationally accepted.

Fig. 39   One of Lucio Fontana's sculptures from *Spatial Concept: Nature* (no. 34), showing a mysterious gouge deep in its center.

Biomorphism and Fantasy

Some abstract styles in art were inspired by elements in the natural world, including water, clouds, plants, rocks, human and animal anatomy, microscopic organisms, and even planets. Interpreting their sources imaginatively, artists such as Jean Arp, Joan Miró, and Henry Moore developed organic, quasi-abstract forms (called "biomorphs") that can suggest many possible images or subjects. The Surrealists introduced the idea of fusion, which meant combining disparate sources (a human figure with a mountain, for example, or a bird with an amoeba) to create fantastic and intriguing hybrid forms. They also favored the idea of metamorphosis, which meant portraying their subjects in the process of developing into something else. Such evocative sculptures depend largely on the viewers' curiosity and ability to invent their own interpretations of these unusual forms. ■

Fig. 38   Biomorphic bronzes by Barbara Hepworth (no. 38) and Henry Moore (no. 40).

31 JACQUES LIPCHITZ
Figure, 1926–30, cast 1958–61

Bronze [edition of 8], 85⅜ x 38½ x 29¼ in. (216.8 x 97.7 x 74.3 cm)
Gift of Joseph H. Hirshhorn, 1966 (66.3101)

Inspired by unusual rock formations on the Brittany coast—huge boulders eroded into fantastic, precariously balanced shapes—Lipchitz translated their forms into a small abstract sculpture in his Paris studio. When a collector commissioned an enlarged version, Lipchitz simplified the composition further, partly to express his admiration for the bold forms and expressive power of African tribal carvings. The linear components of *Figure* resemble stylized legs and arms, while their curves may suggest the female gender. The massive oval head with mesmeric, staring eyes dominates the sculpture and commands the viewer's attention. Although elegantly composed, these abstract forms have a rather intimidating effect.

32 JOAN MIRÓ
Lunar Bird, 1944–46, enlarged and cast 1966–67

Bronze [1/7], 89⅜ x 88½ x 58¼ in. (207 x 204.9 x 147.8 cm)
Gift of Joseph H. Hirshhorn, 1972 (72.204)

A leading Surrealist artist, Miró created works intended to intrigue, astonish, and stimulate. Such surprises were meant to remind us of the importance of dreams and imagination as antidotes to the dreary realities of daily life. Miró's fantastic creature, *Lunar Bird*, is a contradiction in terms. The moon has no birds, and terrestrial ones by definition are usually small, lightweight, and feathered, with thin legs and large wings. But this bird is smooth-skinned and enormous, with wings too small to lift its massive body and elephantine legs into flight. The hybrid animal resembles a bull as much as a bird and seems both playful and sinister. The head is crowned with a crescent, symbol of the moon and spiritual matters, which suggests that Miró's "bird" flies more with its mind than its body.

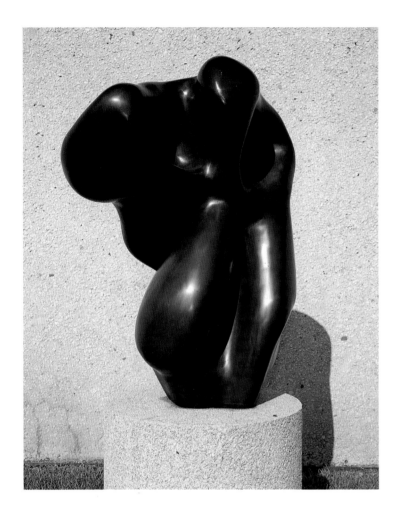 

33 JEAN ARP

Evocation of a Form: Human, Lunar, Spectral,
1950, enlarged and cast 1957

Bronze [1/3], 45½ x 32⅜ x 33½ in. (115.5 x 82.3 x 85 cm)
Gift of Joseph H. Hirshhorn, 1966 (66.107)

In 1916, inspired by forms and growth patterns in the natural world, Arp invented the new style of organic abstraction that would later be adopted by Surrealists and other artists. Believing that hard-edged styles of geometric abstraction (see nos. 45–49) were too cerebral and remote from most people's perceptions, Arp hoped that organic sculptural forms would evoke the dynamic processes of the universe. He believed that images of natural transformations might offer encouraging metaphors for the ever-changing challenges of modern life. Arp used forms allusively, expecting that the viewer would devise personal interpretations of the work. Seen from various angles, this abstract sculpture suggests a muscular male torso, the moon's cratered surface, and the amorphous ectoplasm of a ghostly apparition.

34 LUCIO FONTANA

Spatial Concept: Nature, 1959–60, cast 1965

Bronze [1/3], height 29 to 36⅝ in., diameter 35 to 43⅜ in.
(height 73.7 to 93 cm, diameter 88.9 to 110.1 cm)
Gift of Joseph H. Hirshhorn, 1980 (80.21 and 80.160–163). See also fig. 39.

These five spheres were originally modeled in clay, a medium that allowed the artist to manipulate them in evocatively different ways. One globe appears to be split nearly in half by a horizontal groove, one is only partially cut, another is slashed across the top, and two have holes dug out of the top. Although most bronze casts are hollow, these are solid (each weighs about 300 pounds). Their substantial mass implies that a great force of nature—perhaps a violent storm or an attack by animals—was needed to create such gouges. The artist intended the works to be seen in natural settings (he once installed them in an open field, another time among trees), and he expected their placement to vary in relation to one another depending on the site. Resembling extraterrestrial pods or giant gaping eyeballs, these sculptures convey a sense of life and its fragility.

35 HENRY MOORE
Upright Motive No. 1: Glenkiln Cross, 1955–56

Bronze [edition of 6], 131³/₈ x 38³/₈ x 36 in. (333.6 x 97.4 x 96.6 cm)
Gift of Joseph H. Hirshhorn, 1966 (66.3629). See also figs. 22 and 30.

Having worked extensively on reclining horizontal figures
in preceding years (see no. 15), Moore was excited by a
commission to create a sculpture for the courtyard of the
Olivetti Building, a low-lying horizontal structure in Milan.
Enjoying the chance to explore a different direction, the artist
made thirteen small maquettes of abstract vertical biomorphic
forms, each subtly different. Five were eventually enlarged,
but none went to Milan because Olivetti wanted to place the
artwork in a parking lot and Moore felt that "cars and
sculptures really do not go well together." This composition
had no specific title until the first bronze cast was purchased
and placed on the Glenkiln Farm Estate in Scotland. Moore
then discovered that from a distance it reminded him of the
medieval Celtic stone crosses that still survive in parts of the
British landscape.

36 DIMITRI HADZI
Helmet V, 1959–61

Bronze [1/4], 77¹/₄ x 37¹/₈ x 32⁵/₈ in. (196 x 94.1 x 82.7 cm)
Gift of Joseph H. Hirshhorn, 1966 (66.2306). See also fig. 33.

In 1946, inspired by an exhibition of sculptures by Henry Moore,
American-born Hadzi adopted biomorphic forms for his own
work. After participating in a competition for a monument for
the Auschwitz concentration camp in 1958, he was motivated
to start a series of sculptures on the theme of weaponry and
armor—a subject with fearful relevance during the Cold War.
Helmet V suggests an enormous warrior with empty (but
somehow staring) eyes and a body consisting of tendrils
ominously reminiscent of a huge jellyfish.

37 HENRY MOORE
Standing Figure: Knife Edge (Working Model),
1961, cast 1961–62

Bronze [6/7], 63¾ x 26 x 23½ in. (162 x 66 x 59.7 cm)
Gift of Joseph H. Hirshhorn, 1966 (66.3653)

Like *Three-Piece No. 3: Vertebrae* (no. 41), this work was
inspired by the animal bones that Moore collected and kept
in his studios. Attracted to the shape of a small fragment, he
embedded it in plaster to make a tiny model, which his
assistants enlarged in plaster and cast in bronze. The thin edge
of the bone fragment contrasts with the wider mass on the
opposite side, suggesting, from some angles, a strange figure
standing or turning.

38 BARBARA HEPWORTH

Figure for Landscape, 1960, cast 1965

Bronze [2/7], 106½ x 53⅞ x 28⅜ in. (273 x 137.8 x 72 cm)
Gift of Joseph H. Hirshhorn, 1966 (66.2450). See also fig. 38.

Hepworth, like her friend Henry Moore, created sculptural forms derived from nature, and she was especially inspired by the sea-washed rocks near her home in Cornwall. In the Hirshhorn's sculpture the abstract shape suggests a standing figure, perhaps robed and hooded, yet entirely hollow inside. Paradoxically, the interior space becomes more important than the enveloping bronze. As the viewer's gaze is pulled inside, where the surfaces are subtly textured, the openings allow the surrounding landscape to become part of the artwork. Even sunlight creates varied effects. At dawn, for example, the dark exterior acquires a golden rosy glow (as seen here); later, in the intense clarity of midday, the inner surface is surprisingly green (as illustrated on p. 60).

39 REUBEN NAKIAN

Goddess of the Golden Thighs, 1964–65, cast 1969–74

Bronze [2/4], 102¼ x 141¾ x 66½ in. (259.8 x 360 x 168.9 cm)
Gift of Joseph H. Hirshhorn, 1974 (74.3)

An erudite artist, Nakian wanted to link modern sculptural styles with traditional classical motifs (see also *The Rape of Lucrece*, no. 50). *Goddess of the Golden Thighs* alludes to the divine embodiment of female sensuality, personified in Greco-Roman mythology by Aphrodite, Leda, and Circe, as well as biblical temptresses such as Salomé. Unlike Lachaise's *Standing Woman* (no. 9), Nakian's sculpture is abstract, with a massive torso and cylindrical forms suggesting the outspread legs and arms of a larger-than-life goddess. The bronze's surface is rough and uneven, as if the goddess is fiercely sensual or was savagely treated.

40 HENRY MOORE

Three-Piece Reclining Figure No. 2: Bridge Prop,
1963, cast 1964

Bronze [2/7], 49½ x 78⅞ x 51⅞ in. (115.2 x 251.5 x 131.7 cm)
Gift of Joseph H. Hirshhorn, 1966 (66.3656).
See also fig. 38.

41 HENRY MOORE

Three-Piece No. 3: Vertebrae (Working Model),
1968, cast 1969 ▶

Bronze [2/9], 40¾ x 93 x 48 in. (103.6 x 236.1 x 122 cm)
Joseph H. Hirshhorn Bequest, 1981 (86.3278).
See also fig. 33.

For nearly sixty years, Moore explored many variations on the theme of a reclining figure (see also nos. 15 and 42). Initially inspired by ancient sources, such as Greek and Pre-Columbian sculptures of recumbent gods, the artist used the reclining figure to make analogies between human and other forms in nature, particularly rocky or mountainous landscapes. In *Bridge Prop*, Moore defined the figure as sleek, organic, abstract forms. The title refers to both the subject's pose (propped up on one arm) and Moore's later perception that the sculpture reminded him of a view under Waterloo Bridge in London. *Vertebrae* expresses Moore's passion for collecting bones; in his studios were samples ranging from a small bird skeleton to an elephant's skull. Without referring to any particular type of bone, *Vertebrae* evokes the arbitrary patterns of fossils.

71

42 HENRY MOORE

Two-Piece Reclining Figure: Points, 1969–70, cast 1973

Bronze [4/8], 89³⁄₈ x 147¹⁄₈ x 72⁷⁄₈ in. (227 x 373.7 x 185.2 cm)
Gift of Joseph H. Hirshhorn, 1974 (74.1)

Like numbers 40 and 41, this sculpture consists of organic forms that contrast with the figurative mode of Moore's early works (see no. 15). It can be viewed as one figure in two parts or as two figures (male and female). The shapes have a dynamic vitality, appearing to twist and squirm, while the element on the right thrusts suggestively at the one opposite. Such vigor, with its sexual undertones, expresses Moore's unflagging passion for art and life, even at age seventy-two.

43 RICHARD HUNT

Large Hybrid, 1971

Bronze [1/3], 100½ x 42 x 25¼ in. (255.2 x 106.7 64.2 cm)
Gift of Max Robinson, 1984 (84.15)
Photographed in The White House garden

This bronze belongs to a series of sculptures in which the artist combined geometric shapes with free-flowing organic forms (hence the name "hybrid"). Here, the upper part of the geometric columnar base is transformed into a birdlike creature that appears to spread its wings as if to fly. The abstract image of an upward and outward-reaching metamorphosis conveys an impression of growth and liberation.

44 WILLIAM TUCKER

Gymnast III, 1984–85

Bronze [1/4], 88¾ x 60¼ x 36⅛ in. (225.4 x 153 x 91.8 cm)
Regents Collections Acquisition Program with Matching Funds from the
Joseph H. Hirshhorn Purchase Fund, 1987 (87.13)

In the early 1980s, Tucker created a series of abstract sculptures that refer to human anatomy and athletic movement. The shape of the Hirshhorn's sculpture suggests the directional movement of a gymnast's leap or tumble but does not describe an individual body. The diagonal energy of the form is offset by the sheer weight of the sculpture, as if to imply that athletic endeavor is forever a struggle against gravity.

Geometry and Rational Construction

In the early twentieth century, technological inventions such as the telephone, automobile, airplane, radio, mass-production factories, and other miracles of modern engineering changed society at an amazing rate and inspired hopes for a better future in the so-called Machine Age. The Italian Futurists, Russian Constructivists, and many other artists replaced traditional realism with clear geometric forms assembled into rational structures, often with smooth surfaces intended to emulate the appearance of machines. These innovators believed that their constructive techniques and styles of measured geometry were more appropriate to the modern technological era and could transcend the limitations and divisions of different cultures to become an international visual language. Some artists hoped that the beauty, clarity, and universality of geometric abstraction would help propagate a more rational and objective society. In the early years, artists streamlined and restructured the human body, while later they preferred to compose works of pure abstraction without allusion to any particular subject.

Simultaneously, many artists became interested in using a wide variety of materials. While traditional techniques such as carving stone and casting bronze continued, twentieth-century sculptors often turned to new materials deemed more relevant to an industrial and scientific epoch. In the 1920s and 1930s some artists began to construct sculptures from prefabricated or found pieces of iron, steel, copper, aluminum, and other metals, which they soldered, welded, or bolted together. That practice became widespread in the 1950s and 1960s, especially for outdoor works. Many sculptors, such as Alexander Calder and Claes Oldenburg, often initiated a large project by making a small model (maquette) from which technicians would fabricate an enlarged version. Others, such as David Smith and Anthony Caro, valued a more spontaneous method, cutting and constructing their works improvisationally. Some artists emphasized the industrial nature of their work by leaving visible welds and raw metal, while others painted or burnished the steel surfaces for highly refined effects. ∎

Fig. 41   A detail of David Smith's *Cubi XII* (no. 52) shows the sun's light reflected in the swirling linear patterns of the steel surface.

Fig. 40   Alexander Calder's *Two Discs* (no. 53) installed near the entrance to the Hirshhorn Museum.

45 ALEXANDER ARCHIPENKO

The Gondolier, 1914, reconstructed 1949–50,
enlarged and cast 1957

Bronze [2/6], 72⅛ x 24¾ x 15⅝ in. (181 x 63 x 39.8 cm)
Gift of Joseph H. Hirshhorn, 1966 (66.77)
Photographed in The White House garden

Archipenko's choice of subject—the Venetian boatmen famous
for their traditional costume—allowed him to make a point
about how a modern figure sculpture should look. Rejecting
picturesque details, he emphasized instead a simplified basic
structure for the body, and he streamlined forms into smoothly
tapering tubes. In particular, he combined the man's leg and oar
into a single element, the diagonal energy of which suggests
potential motion; accordingly, the body becomes analogous to
a rowing machine. Archipenko also smoothed and polished the
bronze surface to a gleaming black sheen that may evoke
spiritual purity as well as technological sophistication. When
the sculpture was exhibited in Paris in 1914, its geometric,
mechanistic forms prompted a newspaper critic to compare
it to a factory chimney. Artists, however, were immediately
impressed by *The Gondolier*, which inspired other conceptual
(rather than descriptive) figural images.

46 PABLO GARGALLO

The Prophet, 1933, cast 1954–68

Bronze [5/7], 92¼ x 29¾ x 19 in. (234.2 x 75.5 x 48.2 cm)
Gift of Joseph H. Hirshhorn, 1972 (72.124). See also figs. 22 and 38.

Trained as an ironworker, Gargallo began in the 1920s to construct small works of welded metal, usually heads of copper, iron, and silver. In 1933 he undertook his largest sculpture, *The Prophet*, which was partly inspired by the welded metal sculptures recently made by his friends Pablo Picasso and Julio González. Such works would later inspire David Smith and other sculptors to use constructivist methods in the 1950s and 1960s (see nos. 47–48, 51–52). The original *Prophet*, which was too delicate to be shown outdoors, was later cast in bronze. This composition started out as a figure of Saint John the Baptist preaching, but it evolved into a more universal image evoking the prophets of many faiths, such as Abraham and Moses, the Buddha, and Mohammed. Rather than the single solid mass

normally used for a human figure, this sculpture consists of interlocking, curved shapes. The contrapuntal rhythm of convex and concave contours creates an optical effect of movement and energy—an apt visual metaphor for the passion engendered by religious belief.

47 DAVID SMITH
Agricola I, 1951–52

Painted steel, 73½ x 55¼ x 24⅝ in. (186.5 x 140.3 x 62.5 cm)
Gift of Joseph H. Hirshhorn, 1966 (66.4638)

Trained as a welder during World War II, Smith became a prominent leader in the development of constructed metal sculptures in the United States during the 1950s and 1960s. Working in upstate New York, he was intrigued by relics of modern industrial machinery, including discarded farm implements. Smith used the disassembled parts to make a series of two dozen sculptures titled *Agricola*, the Latin word for farmer. He fashioned this first one into a whimsically elegant, abstract figure, who stands above his tractor seat and holds a tool in one hand. Later sculptures became increasingly abstract.

48 DAVID SMITH
Pittsburgh Landscape, 1954

Painted steel, 30 x 116¼ x 5½ in. (76 x 295.2 x 14 cm)
Gift of Joseph H. Hirshhorn, 1972 (72.266)

This work was originally created as a guardrail for the terrace outside the house of G. David Thompson, a collector of modern art and president of Pittsburgh Steel in the 1950s. The forms and lines in the abstract composition suggest the rhythms and patterns of a dynamic landscape viewed from a distance or perhaps from above (Smith was known to appreciate aerial perspectives). The sculptor defined elements in the landscape as flowing boundary and horizon lines, geometric roofs, trees and lakes, and the passage of sun and moon, which are interpreted lyrically.

49 ALEXANDER CALDER
Six Dots over a Mountain, 1956

Painted steel, 156½ x 212¼ x 79⅝ in. (397.5 x 539.1 x 202.2 cm)
Gift of Joseph H. Hirshhorn, 1966 (66.790)
See also frontispiece and fig. 3.

Attracted to the Surrealist emphasis on imagination and fantasy, Calder was inspired by biomorphic forms in the works of Arp and Miró and by the geometric structure and primary colors of Piet Mondrian's paintings. In 1930, Calder invented kinetic sculptures later called "mobiles." Those delicate constructions were usually suspended indoors from ceilings or walls; Calder also made standing mobiles, in which the moving elements balance atop a stable base. In the 1950s he made these stabile-mobiles on a larger scale in sturdy steel for outdoor display. Inspired by diverse structures in the cosmos (from planetary orbits to spiders' webs), Calder understood his sculptures as analogous to nature's own systems: ordered yet spontaneously changing. *Six Dots over a Mountain* suggests clouds or birds circulating near a mountain peak. Moved by the wind's fluctuating rhythms, the work interacts with the forces of nature—an abstract metaphor for the ceaseless changes of life. On sunny days the sculpture acquires another, ephemeral dimension in the changing pattern of shadows on the ground.

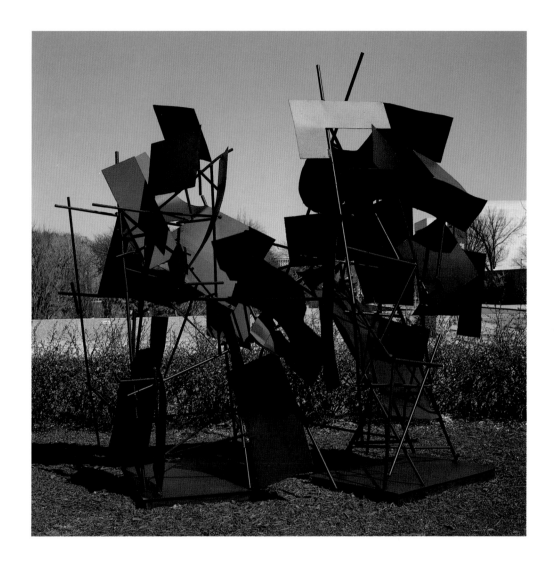

50 REUBEN NAKIAN
The Rape of Lucrece, 1955–58

Painted steel, 141¼ x 154⅝ x 87⅛ in. (358.8 x 392.8 x 221.3 cm)
Gift of Joseph H. Hirshhorn, 1974 (74.2)

Nakian turned to monumental sculpture in 1954–55 with the goal of combining traditional classical subjects with modern style. This sculpture refers to the ancient Roman legend of a virtuous aristocratic woman named Lucretia (Lucrece in Shakespeare's poem) who was raped by the king's son, Sextus Tarquinius. Lucrece committed suicide, and her husband sought revenge by forcing Sextus into exile. Rather than create a literal image, Nakian suggested in abstract terms the confrontation between the strong-willed Lucrece and her attacker. The sculpture's composition—multiple black steel plates grouped in two sections, locked firmly together by welded rods—acts as a metaphor for a grim struggle in a confined space.

51 DAVID SMITH
Voltri XV, 1962

Steel, 89⅞ x 77¼ x 22⅝ in. (228.1 x 196.1 x 57.4 cm)
Gift of Joseph H. Hirshhorn, 1966 (66.4643)

In 1962, at the peak of his career, Smith was invited to create sculptures for display at the Spoleto Music Festival in Italy, and he went to work in the recently abandoned steel factories at Voltri, near Genoa. Finding a tremendous supply of scrap metal, mostly flat pieces of sheet steel, Smith cut and welded those fragments together at an astounding rate. Assisted by several welders, he made a series of twenty-six geometric sculptures in only thirty days in May and June. Although abstract, *Voltri XV* suggests the image of a sun or moon with passing clouds. Indeed, the sculpture was meant to be seen outdoors, with grass, trees, and sky as part of the sculpture.

52 DAVID SMITH
Cubi XII, 1963

Stainless steel, 109⅝ x 49¼ x 32¼ in. (278.5 x 125.1 x 81.9 cm)
Gift of the Joseph H. Hirshhorn Foundation, 1972 (72.268). See also fig. 41.

From 1961 through 1965, Smith worked on a series of twenty-eight sculptures constructed from square and rectangular hollow blocks (*cubi*) of stainless steel. He intended the shapes and material to contrast and interact with the outdoor landscape. Trees and sky are visible through the central openings and reflected on the sculpture's surface, so that areas sometimes appear pale blue or green. Smith burnished the shiny surface into delicate layers of curving linear patterns that become visible only in certain light conditions. On an overcast day some lines appear as gray swirls, but in bright sunlight other patterns emerge and shine with fiery intensity. Such changes in natural light lend a delicate kinetic quality to *Cubi XII*, even though the sculpture does not actually move.

53 ALEXANDER CALDER
Two Discs, 1965

Painted steel, 306 x 328 x 208 in. (777.3 x 833.2 x 528.3 cm)
Gift of Joseph H. Hirshhorn, 1966 (66.791). See also fig. 40.

In addition to his mobiles (see no. 49), Calder made large stationary works called stabiles. Using heavy industrial metal, he delighted in creating buoyant effects by designing elegant shapes that suggest lightness and movement. Here, tons of steel perch delicately on five tiny "feet" barely four inches long, and the angled legs curve gracefully upward like the trajectory of a balloon or a bird, culminating in the two highest angles that point up to the sky.

54 KENNETH SNELSON
Needle Tower, 1968

Aluminum and stainless steel, 720 x 243½ x 213⅜ in.
(1828.8 x 618.5 x 541.8 cm)
Gift of Joseph H. Hirshhorn, 1974 (74.4)

Inspired by Buckminster Fuller (inventor of the geodesic dome), Snelson adapted engineering principles to devise his own system of tensional structure based on mathematical calculations. Instead of the solid mass and weight traditionally expected of monumental sculptures, the tapering *Needle Tower* is more like a delicate frame or enclosure for space, which is defined in three-dimensional geometric shapes (pyramids, rhomboids, and other polyhedrons). The tubes push and pull in different directions, held together in perfect balance by a single continuous wire threaded through two small holes in the ends of each tube. As tall as a five-story building, *Needle Tower* is made from aviation-quality aluminum tubes and stainless steel wire, thus making it lightweight enough for three installers to lift. The tower rests only on the thin rims of three tubes; yet the structure is so well designed that it withstands severe storms. While its technology is fascinating in itself, the sculpture also conveys a metaphysical message. Standing inside the sculpture and looking up, the viewer discovers that the tubes create the shape of a star (with all its astronomical, astrological, and religious associations). The star contour is repeated in diminishing sizes upward until it disappears into the sky, inviting contemplation of an infinite cosmos or spiritual domain.

Looking up the interior of *Needle Tower*

55 CLAES OLDENBURG
Geometric Mouse: Variation 1, Scale A, 1971

Painted steel and aluminum [3/6], 106¼ x 143⅝ x 94⅜ in.
(267.8 x 364.7 x 242.2 cm). Museum Purchase, 1974 (75.1)

In the 1960s, Pop artists rejected serious subjects and abstract styles, which they considered pretentious and elitist. Instead, they preferred familiar objects from daily life and popular culture. Oldenburg likes to enlarge mundane images for public places, turning items such as a lipstick or a fan into the subject of "important" art. In this sculpture he adapted geometric abstraction to accommodate the image of a mouse's head. Although some people think the sculpture refers to a famous cartoon character, the artist described *Geometric Mouse* as having multiple associations. The two round ears refer to old reel-to-reel movie projectors, while the structure echoes the false-façade houses built for stage and movie productions, with the eyelids resembling window shades or shutters. The artist also called the image a self-portrait. The angle of the head reclines as if the mouse is just waking from sleep. Awakening seems difficult, as the eyelids are held down by chains and circles on the ground; these elements have been likened to tears or monocles, each with its connotation of sadness or shortsightedness. Oldenburg made many versions of his mouse in different colors and sizes, with the ear diameter ranging from nine inches to nineteen feet.

56 ANTHONY CARO
Monsoon Drift, 1975

Steel, 123¼ x 207 x 41 in. (321.9 x 525.7 x 104.1 cm)
Museum Purchase, 1976 (76.94)

As an assistant to Henry Moore for two years, Caro learned about organic sculptural forms related to nature. Then in 1959 he was inspired by the abstract geometry and industrial methods of David Smith's sculptures. In developing his own style, Caro has emphasized the importance of working improvisationally. Without preliminary studies, he begins by arranging pieces of metal in various configurations until he discovers the right composition—not an easy task when the individual steel elements are large and heavy. Here, an underlying geometric structure of I-beams supports an undulating curtain or wave of metal. Although Caro started *Monsoon Drift* with no particular subject in mind, the resulting sinuous shapes evoke crashing waves, so he titled this sculpture for ocean currents around the Indian subcontinent.

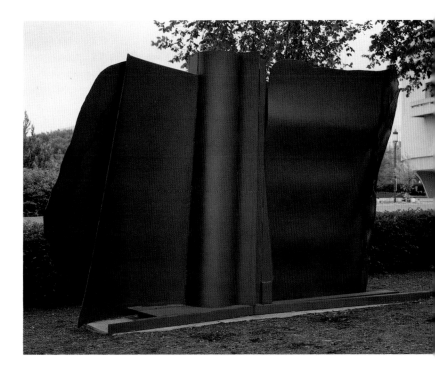

57 TONY SMITH
Throwback, 1976–79

Painted aluminum [1/3], 81¼ x 155⅞ x 95⅝ in. (206.5 x 395.9 x 242.6 cm)
Museum Purchase, 1980 (80.3). See also fig.27.

The artist first created this composition as a small cardboard maquette measuring only 14 x 32 x 16 inches, which he enlarged to full size in plywood and then had fabricated in aluminum by technicians. Smith chose the title because the work was a throwback to earlier traditions, particularly the reclining human figure found in the sculptures of many cultures, including ancient Greece and Pre-Columbian Mexico, and in the organic abstractions of Henry Moore (see nos. 15 and 40–42). *Throwback* epitomizes pure abstraction, made for the beauty of its geometric forms and their interactions, which can be fully appreciated only when seen dynamically from different angles. As the viewer walks around the work, its appearance changes surprisingly from a complex zigzag arrangement of octahedrons and tetrahedrons to simpler diagonals and then back again in a horizontal motion. In changing light the matte black paint makes some elements appear darker than others, creating illusions of depth and solidity.

58 ELLSWORTH KELLY
Untitled, 1986

Stainless steel, 75 x 30 x 107 in. (190.5 x 330.2 x 348 cm)
Museum Purchase, 1986 (86.5897). See also fig. 27.

Known primarily as a painter of elegant abstract forms in sensuous colors, Kelly has also sculpted for many years. While chatting with another artist in 1959, he cut and folded the paper top of a take-out coffee container, making its rimmed edges rock on the tabletop. This simple act led to a series of sculptures of curved forms that he called "rockers" (referring partly to children's hobbyhorses). Kelly made three from 1963 to 1968 and three more in 1982, followed four years later by the Hirshhorn's example. Each version consists of two circular or circular-wedge forms joined along a single "spine." By adjusting the radius of the circles and the angle of their juncture, Kelly created an array of perfectly balanced structures.

Contemporary Views

By the 1980s the extraordinary ideas and styles that had transformed modern art in the early and mid-twentieth century had begun to wane. After decades dominated by abstraction, a new generation reacted against that emphasis on form and style. Sometimes called postmodernists, these artists have taken a wider and more inclusive view of art history. For subject matter, many have turned to the familiar imagery of the human figure to reach a broad audience and express an endless array of ideas, emotions, and moods. A few sculptors have even reintroduced the older traditions of narrative, allegory, and symbolism. Favoring "art about art," some artists quote from the masterpieces of bygone times. Others make critiques of current events or attitudes, while certain sculptors portray items from daily life. Never merely a literal description, such object-sculptures usually pose a question or convey a commentary, which is often humorous but may range the gamut from indifference to censure. Today, virtually any subject is feasible, any interpretation is tenable, and any material or technique is appropriate. ■

Fig. 43   Detail of central figures in Juan Muñoz's *Conversation Piece* (no. 63).

Fig. 42   The Hirshhorn Museum's plaza and fountain at night, with sculpture by Barry Flanagan (no. 60).

59 ARMAN

Eros, Inside Eros, 1986

Bronze [1/2], 33⅝ x 17¼ x 20⅛ in. (85.4 x 43.8 x 51.1 cm)
Joseph H. Hirshhorn Bequest, by Exchange, 1987 (87.10)

From the outset of his career in the 1960s, Arman fostered
an irreverent perspective toward established traditions. He
sometimes threw artistic "tantrums" in which he destroyed
objects (such as antique furniture or musical instruments) and
used the fragments to make sculptures. His work elicits in the
viewer a sense of shock at the destruction of a valued older
object as a means to create new art. Fascinated by the insides
of things, Arman began cutting up objects in 1962. Here, he
applied that violent approach to art history by slicing the
plaster cast of a classical torso, specifically the god of love and
sexuality, and casting the pieces in bronze. The implications of
the nothingness inside are both amusing and disturbing.

60 BARRY FLANAGAN
The Drummer, 1989–90

Bronze [2/7], 96 x 68 x 36 in. (243.8 x 172.7 x 91.4 cm)
Joseph H. Hirshhorn Purchase Fund and Joseph H. Hirshhorn Bequest Fund,
1995 (95.4). See also fig. 42.

Animals have long served as subjects for art, from ancient
symbols of royal or religious power to naturalistic and romantic
studies of wild animals in nineteenth-century illustrations. In
contrast to those earlier depictions of regal lions and horses,
Flanagan has chosen to portray wild hares invested with human
characteristics. The artist has never explained his
anthropomorphic images, but for many viewers the sculptures
evoke a cartoon character fondly known for eluding persecution
with ease and humor. Flanagan's hares seem to have a similar
insouciance, as they perform various stunts, such as running,
leaping, or fighting. Here, while standing atop a pyramid, the
hare beats a drum. Perhaps it is simply expressing a child's joy in
a favorite toy. Or, if the pyramid represents a mountain, the
figure may be interpreted as a lighthearted symbol of triumph.

61 JUDITH SHEA
Post-Balzac, 1991

Bronze [2/3], 98½ x 28½ x 28½ in. (250.2 x 72.9 x 72.9 cm)
Museum Purchase, 1991 (91.20)
Photographed in The White House garden. See also fig. 31.

Knowing that Rodin's *Monument to Balzac* (no. 3) embodied
certain beliefs and ideals, Shea used it as a point of comparison.
Rodin's sculpture made the famous writer appear larger than
life, a creative genius rising above ordinary events. In *Post-
Balzac*, Shea depicts only the writer's robe without the man
inside it. Her sculpture offers a wry and somewhat sad
commentary on the spiritual emptiness and disillusionment
of the modern era ("XX" inscribed on the base indicates the
century). The artist insinuates that our concerns are too often
focused on outer appearances rather than inner meaning, and,
as a result, vacuous pomposity has replaced human substance.

62 TONY CRAGG
Subcommittee, 1991

Steel [edition of 4], 100½ x 74¼ x 64½ in. (255.1 x 188.5 x 163.8 cm)
Gift of the Frederick R. Weisman Art Foundation and Museum Purchase, 1992 (92.10)

Like the Pop artists of the 1960s (see Oldenburg, no. 55), Cragg favors the accessible imagery of daily life as the means for conveying an idea or opinion. Unlike some artists of the 1980s and 1990s, he refrains from political topics, preferring instead to present ordinary subjects with wry, satiric, or absurdist implications of universal appeal. In this sculpture he has portrayed an old-fashioned rack of worn rubber stamps, an image familiar to anyone who has worked in an office or tried to obtain a public permit. *Subcommittee* serves as a humorous and ironic symbol for bureaucracies everywhere and therefore is a singularly appropriate image for Washington, D.C. By making this work in low-grade steel, which rusts outdoors, Cragg added a further sly comment on the archaic slowness of bureaucracy.

63 JUAN MUÑOZ

Conversation Piece, 1994–95

Bronze [1/1], 66½ x 244¾ x 321⅛ in.
(168.9 x 621.7 x 815.7 cm)
Museum Purchase, 1995 (95.5). See also fig. 43.

Well versed in the history of art, Muñoz creates tableaux of one or more figures situated in ways that suggest isolation or alienation. Since 1989, Muñoz has worked with the Renaissance concept of a "conversation piece": compositions in which several figures interact with one another and with their setting to generate a mood or narrative. The life-size figures stand on the ground without a pedestal, inviting viewers to become part of the drama. Initially inspired by a ventriloquist's dummy, the characters resemble stuffed toys, particularly punching bags or the round-bottomed clowns that bounce back up after being

hit. The three central figures are enmeshed in an emotional confrontation, although the story is not specified. One protagonist aggressively pushes the central personage, whose body curves back in recoil; another leans in closely as if to murmur. Each posture and gesture suggests urgency and tension, concern and empathy. Two ancillary figures lean as if seeking to move into the drama, but their desire for involvement is frustrated by their legless shape. Muñoz's work invites various interpretations but is never fully explained, leaving a sense of speculation and mystery.

Index of Artists